DON'T BE THE NEXT VICTIM

50 WAYS TO PROTECT YOURSELF AGAINST CRIME.

Recommended By
Citizens Against Crime®

Copyright 1993, Guardian Press
All Rights Reserved.
Printed in the United States of America.
No part of this book may be used or reproduced in any manner whatsoever without written permission, except in the case of brief quotations embodied in critical articles or reviews.

ISBN 0-9632355-0-8

The information contained in this book was obtained from various outside sources, including, but not limited to, federal, state and local law enforcement officials and crime prevention experts. We believe it to be reliable and accurate. However, we do not warrant the accuracy or reliability of the information contained herein. Further, Guardian Press makes no guarantees of results from the use of information contained herein. We assume no liability in connection with either the information contained in this book or the crime prevention suggestions made. Moreover, we would caution that it cannot be assumed that every acceptable crime prevention procedure is contained in this book. Obviously, abnormal, unusual or individual circumstances may require further or additional procedures.

For ordering information, call
Citizens Against Crime, Inc.
1-800-466-1010

DON'T BE THE NEXT VICTIM

50 WAYS TO PROTECT YOURSELF AGAINST CRIME.

Written and Edited by
Richard W. Eaves
and
Steven E. Watson

Guardian Press

ACKNOWLEDGMENTS

Guardian Press would like to thank the following organizations whose cooperation and suggestions helped make this book possible.

In alphabetical order:

- Bellaire, Texas, Police Department, Crime Prevention Unit
- Citizens Against Crime, Inc.
- Federal Bureau of Investigation, U.S. Department of Justice
- Harris County, Texas, Sheriff's Department
- Houston-Galveston Area Council
- Houston Police Department, Crime Prevention Unit
- Office of the Attorney General of the State of Texas
- Office of the Governor of the State of Texas
- Texas Crime Prevention Institute, Southwest Texas State University
- Texas Criminal Justice Division
- Texas Law Enforcement Assistance Division

Special Editorial Assistance Provided by
Citizens Against Crime, Inc.

CONTENTS

INTRODUCTION 1

PROTECTING YOURSELF IN THE HOME 3

1. KNOW WHO'S AT THE DOOR BEFORE YOU OPEN IT. 4
2. DON'T DISCUSS YOUR DAILY SCHEDULE OR ROUTINE WITH STRANGERS. 7
3. MAKE IT LOOK LIKE YOU'RE HOME EVEN WHEN YOU'RE GONE. 9
4. MAKE YOUR HOME AS VISIBLE AS POSSIBLE, NIGHT AND DAY. 11
5. FORTIFY DOORS AND WINDOWS WITH EXTRA LOCKS. 13
6. INSTALL AN ALARM SYSTEM. 16
7. MARK ALL VALUABLES WITH IDENTIFYING NUMBERS OR SYMBOLS. 18
8. DON'T TRY TO DEFEND YOUR PROPERTY AT THE RISK OF PERSONAL SAFETY. 20
9. GET INVOLVED WITH YOUR NEIGHBORHOOD WATCH PROGRAM. 22
10. KNOW HOW TO IDENTIFY SUSPICIOUS ACTIVITIES AND HOW TO REPORT THEM. 24
11. BE ALERT TO THE DANGERS OF RAPE IN YOUR HOME. 29

PROTECTION IN AND AROUND YOUR CAR 31

12. CHECK OUT THE SCENE BEFORE GETTING IN YOUR CAR. 32

13	KNOW WHERE YOU'RE GOING BEFORE YOU LEAVE.	36
14	TELL A FRIEND OR RELATIVE WHERE YOU'RE GOING AND WHEN YOU'LL RETURN.	38
15	PLAN YOUR TRIPS FOR THE DAYLIGHT HOURS WHENEVER POSSIBLE.	40
16	AVOID CONFRONTATIONS WITH OTHER MOTORISTS.	42
17	BE AS INCONSPICUOUS AS POSSIBLE.	44
18	MAKE YOUR CAR HARD TO STEAL.	48
19	MAKE YOUR CAR EVEN HARDER TO STEAL.	50
20	DON'T LEAVE AN OPEN INVITATION IN YOUR CAR.	53
21	KNOW WHAT TO DO IF YOUR CAR BREAKS DOWN.	55
22	GUARD AGAINST CAR-JACKING.	58
23	KNOW THE LOCATION OF "SAFE PLACES".	60
24	DON'T TAKE UNNECESSARY RISKS.	63
25	ALWAYS BE PREPARED FOR AN EMERGENCY.	67

PRECAUTIONS TO TAKE WHILE TRAVELING ... 71

26	DON'T LET YOUR CAR GIVE AWAY THE FACT THAT YOU'RE A TOURIST.	72
27	UNLOAD YOUR CAR WHEN YOU STOP EACH NIGHT.	74
28	AT AIRPORTS, TAKE SPECIAL PRECAUTIONS WITH PURSES AND LUGGAGE.	76
29	SECURE YOUR PURSE BEFORE YOU FALL ASLEEP ON A BUS OR PLANE.	79

30	DON'T LEAVE VALUABLES UNATTENDED WHILE YOU PLAY.	81
31	NEVER LEAVE VALUABLES IN YOUR HOTEL ROOM WHEN YOU'RE NOT THERE.	83
32	FOLLOW ALL SECURITY WARNINGS IN HOTELS.	84
33	DON'T CARRY A LOT OF CASH WITH YOU.	85
34	TAKE SPECIAL PRECAUTIONS WITH CREDIT CARDS.	86

PRECAUTIONS TO TAKE IN THE WORKPLACE ... 87

35	USE CAR POOLS AND VAN POOLS WHENEVER POSSIBLE.	88
36	EXERCISE GREAT CARE ON PUBLIC TRANSPORTATION SYSTEMS.	90
37	BE EXTRA CAREFUL IN PARKING GARAGES, STAIRWELLS AND ELEVATORS.	92
38	KEEP YOUR VALUABLES LOCKED UP AT THE OFFICE.	95
39	KEEP BUSINESS DOORS LOCKED WHENEVER POSSIBLE.	96
40	TRY TO AVOID KEEPING A LOT OF CASH ON HAND AT YOUR BUSINESS.	97
41	VARY YOUR ROUTINE WHEN MAKING BANK DEPOSITS.	99
42	MAKE SURE EVERYBODY KNOWS WHAT TO DO IN CASE OF A ROBBERY.	100
43	MAKE YOUR BUSINESS AS VISIBLE AS POSSIBLE.	102

PRECAUTIONS TO TAKE WHILE SHOPPING ... 103

| 44 | LOOK BEFORE YOU PARK YOUR CAR. | 104 |

45	DON'T SHOP TILL YOU DROP YOUR GUARD.	106
46	BE ALERT TO ANYONE FOLLOWING YOU OUT OF THE STORE.	108
47	PREPARE TO GET IN YOUR CAR BEFORE YOU LEAVE THE STORE.	110
48	MAKE YOURSELF A MOVING TARGET.	112
49	KEEP YOUR PURSE ZIPPED SHUT AND YOUR HAND ON THE ZIPPER.	114
50	BEWARE OF A FALSE SENSE OF SECURITY FROM SELF-DEFENSE WEAPONS.	117

INTRODUCTION

No one has to tell you that America is in the grips of a crime wave of unprecedented proportions. You see it each night on the news and read about it every morning in the newspaper.

But the news we actually get about crime can be misleading. We only see and hear about the unusual, the senseless or sensational. Crime has become so commonplace, so much a part of our daily lives, that most of it isn't even news anymore. It is simply a fact of our existence.

In some ways crime is a lot like the weather. Everybody's talking about it, but nobody's doing much about it. It's doubtful that anybody can do anything about it, at least in the near future. Most experts agree that crime is a result of deep-rooted social ills such as poor education, a breakdown in the family unit and drug abuse, all of which are too serious to cure overnight.

Crime has stretched the criminal justice system to the breaking point. Prisons, overflowing with criminals, are little more than revolving doors. Criminals know that they won't serve long sentences, for there simply is no place to put them.

Police and law enforcement officials have had their positions overrun by an army of criminals with both superior numbers and firepower.

So who's going to protect you? For the most part, you're going to have to provide for your own protection. The police simply can't be everywhere at once. And even when they make arrests, the arrested party is oftentimes back on the street even before the paperwork is done.

The burden of protecting yourself and your family rests squarely on your shoulders. It's a heavy burden indeed, but not an impossible one.

Criminals usually seek out the easiest, most attractive target possible. They seldom have to work hard to find one. Many people become easy prey simply because they assume that they will not be the victim, that crime only happens to "the other guy".

If this book does nothing else, hopefully it will make you aware that you can easily become a victim of crime at any time—and that your best defense is the right mix of common sense, concentration and extreme caution.

The person most difficult for a criminal to victimize is one who is constantly on the alert, expecting an attack at any moment. This may sound like paranoia, and we certainly don't advocate taking crime prevention to this extreme. As with most things in our lives, the middle ground is where the most workable solution is usually found. Being alert to the possibilities of crime is far different than constantly living in fear of it.

There's no doubt that crime has greatly disrupted our lives, causing some people to radically change the way they live. No doubt, you too will have to make some changes in order to better protect your life and property. As this book demonstrates, those changes need not be drastic, only well conceived.

PROTECTING YOURSELF IN THE HOME

The old saying that "your home is your castle" couldn't be further from the truth. If your home were indeed a "castle", there would be a moat, a drawbridge and thick stone walls protecting it from intruders. Most homes have no such protection. Only a door with a lock. And as crime statistics bear out, that's no deterrent at all for an accomplished thief.

In fact, most burglars in prison boasted that they could break into a victim's home in less time than it takes to unlock a door with a key! Little wonder that a burglary occurs every 10 seconds in this country.

The suggestions that follow won't stop thieves. But they can help make your home, your family and your possessions less of a target—primarily by making things more difficult for thieves. The harder you make it for criminals to victimize you, the less chance you have of becoming a victim.

1 KNOW WHO'S AT THE DOOR BEFORE YOU OPEN IT.

In 95% of all break-ins, burglars have first "cased the joint". That is, they first checked out the house to determine its potential as a target and the best time to strike.

The easiest way for a thief to get in your home is right through the front door—as your invited guest! It should be a family rule to never open the door to strangers.

But strangers aren't your only worry. Sometimes the thief is a neighbor. In fact, 25% of neighborhood burglaries are committed by a neighbor (often a teenager).

Most burglaries, however, are committed by professionals. And before they break in, they'll usually visit your neighborhood first to check out the possibilities. They may pose as everything from joggers to salesmen.

Everyone is familiar with the typical door-to-door salesman trying to persuade you to buy everything from vacuum cleaners to magazines, to siding and lawn care services. Most of these people are decent, law-abiding citizens trying to make an honest living. Unfortunately, criminals have made them all suspect. Therefore, we must react cautiously to any stranger who appears at our door for any reason.

Anyone who comes into your home has an opportunity to size up your home and its potential as a target. They can scrutinize for dogs, security systems, window and door locks—plus TVs, VCRs, stereos and other valuables that can easily be stolen and quickly converted into cash. In simple terms, if a thief doesn't see it, he's less likely to try to steal it.

WHAT YOU CAN DO:

- Install peepholes and use them. That will allow you to identify who's at the door without having to open it. A fish-eye peephole that covers a field of vision of at least 190° works best since it lets you see anyone crouching below or standing to either side of the peephole.

- Don't ignore strangers at your door. If they think you're not home, they might try to break in. Talk to them through the door. If you feel threatened, call the police. Don't open the door, not even a crack.

- Never let your kids answer the door. It's easy for an intruder to trick a child into letting him inside the house.

- Be wary of uninvited salesmen. It's easy for a thief to pose as a salesman to get you to open your door. Even if you don't let him in, if you open the door wide enough, a quick glance inside will give him an idea of the type of possessions you might have. Worse yet, once you open the door, there's nothing to stop the thief from forcing his way into the home to take what he wants. Including your life.

- Check out repairmen before you let them in. Many times, they're invited right into the home, simply because they're wearing a uniform or displaying identification badges. Of course if you have called for their services, you have less reason to be suspicious. But if they appear at your door unsolicited, be extremely wary. Never let unsolicited service personnel into your home. Instead, ask them to wait outside while you contact their company or organization to confirm their affiliation and reason for being there.

2. DON'T DISCUSS YOUR DAILY SCHEDULE OR ROUTINE WITH STRANGERS.

Most burglars want information that will make it easier to enter your home and make off with your valuables. The easiest way for them to learn about your daily routine is to simply ask. If someone comes to your door or calls you on the phone asking questions that pertain to your schedule, they may be attempting to learn your daily routine—when the home will be vacant and for how long, and whether you're a potential target.

WHAT YOU CAN DO:

- Never give your schedule to people who don't need to know. Sometimes, repairmen or sales people will contact you to set an appointment, suggesting a time in either the morning or evening. It isn't necessary to tell them why you won't be available at the suggested times. Simply tell them that the time that they have suggested is not convenient without going into reasons why. Set all appointments for your convenience and personal safety.

- Never tell strangers you are alone (this includes neighbors you don't know very well).

- Be wary of giving any information to telephone "researchers". Even information that seems innocent can be used by a thief to develop a profile of your daily routine. Burglars want information to determine your vulnerability. It's important to remember that most thieves will choose the easiest target, not the most difficult. Don't help them out by letting them know the most convenient time to strike.

- Never tell anyone except for close neighbors you trust that you're going on a trip. Don't tell the newspaper delivery person, not even the mailman. (It's best to have a neighbor pick up your newspapers and mail and hold them for you until you return). This is not to imply that mail and delivery people are potential burglars, but the fewer people who know of your vacation plans the better.

- Never leave a note on your door advising friends, relatives or repairmen that you're gone.

- Don't discuss your travel plans or routine in public places where you may be overheard (grocery stores, restaurants, beauty salons, department stores, etc.). All a burglar has to do is follow you home to get your address—or if he happens to see the address on your check—he'll know where you live as well as when you'll be gone.

- Remember, it's better to be discreet than to end up being a victim.

3. MAKE IT LOOK LIKE YOU'RE HOME EVEN WHEN YOU'RE GONE.

Whether you're going to be away for an extended vacation or just overnight, it's important to give the appearance that someone is at home. The best way to do that is actually have someone be there, like a trusted friend or relative. However, that is seldom practical or possible, so the next best thing is to create the illusion that you're home.

WHAT YOU CAN DO:

- Provide a close neighbor with your schedule, and if at all possible, the telephone numbers of where you can be reached in case of an emergency. Make sure it's a neighbor you trust completely.

- Ask the neighbor to park a car in your driveway at different times of the day to give the appearance that someone is at home.

- Ask your neighbor to pick up mail and newspapers and hold them until you return. If you provide the neighbor with a key to enter your home to water plants or feed pets, also have the neighbor put mail and newspapers inside your home. Never have them left on your front or rear doorstep. That's a dead giveaway that you're gone.

- Use timers to turn on lights inside the home. Try to set the timers consistent with your schedule. If it doesn't get dark until 8:00 PM, then have the lights come on at that time, not an hour later. If you normally go to bed at 10:00 PM, set the timer to turn the lights off at about that time. It's also important to stagger the timers so that certain lights are coming on as others are going off, to make it look as if someone is moving from room to room.

- Set your radio on timers as well, and turn the volume up loud enough so that it can be heard at your front door.

- Keep your curtains closed tightly or drawn just enough to allow light in for plants. Don't have anything of real value visible if the curtains aren't completely closed.

- If your phone has call forwarding, forward it to your close neighbor if the neighbor is agreeable. That way, calls to your home can be answered. Simply instruct your neighbor to take a message without giving any details of your schedule.

- If you have an answering machine, never leave a message that indicates you are gone.

- Turn down the ring volume on your phone so a burglar can't hear it ring and ring and ring with no one to answer it. Better yet, unplug the phone from the wall jack if possible.

- To be on the safe side, lock your jewelry and other small valuables in a safe deposit box at the bank.

- Have a neighbor mow and water your yard to make it look like someone is at home.

4 MAKE YOUR HOME AS VISIBLE AS POSSIBLE, NIGHT AND DAY.

Homes that are surrounded by high fences and shrubs are most inviting to thieves. And why not? They can go about their business without fear of being seen by passing cars or neighbors. At night, thieves have the cover of darkness to protect them from being spotted. That's why it's important to give your home as much visibility as possible around the clock.

WHAT YOU CAN DO:

- Keep your home brightly illuminated at night. Install low wattage wall washers around exterior walls. It can help discourage burglars from sneaking from window to window trying to find an opening. Decorative landscape lighting also can help fill in shadowy areas around shrubbery. Install floodlights for your back yard. Leave your porch light on at night. A well lit home is one of the best deterrents against burglars.

- If you live on a dark street, try to get the neighbors together and petition the city for streetlights. Well-lighted streets can help discourage criminal activity within the neighborhood.

- Leave a light on inside the house at night. If a burglar sees a light on, he can't be sure if someone is awake inside the house. And that just might make him think twice before breaking in.

- Leave a light on inside your garage. And don't forget to

lock it each night. Lawn mowers, bicycles, cars and other possessions inside unlighted, unlocked garages are easy targets (especially for neighborhood teen-age burglars).

- When it's time to replace your fence, consider giving up some of your privacy in favor of a see-through fence. In yards surrounded by high, solid fences, burglars can do their dirty work without having to worry about being spotted by neighbors.

- Keep your shrubs trimmed to a height of not more than two feet.

- If you live on or near a busy thoroughfare, visibility is critical. Burglars strike 40% more often within three blocks of a major thoroughfare that offers an easy escape route. Nearly 4 out of 10 burglaries happen at corner homes because 2 of the closest neighbors are across the street.

5 FORTIFY DOORS AND WINDOWS WITH EXTRA LOCKS.

Regardless of how many precautions you take, there's still the chance that a burglar has pegged your home as a target. So it's important to make your home as difficult as possible to enter, especially on the ground floor where burglars enter 80% of the time.

There's no way to keep a determined thief from breaking into your home. The only thing you can hope to do is make it more time consuming, which may discourage the burglar to the point he'll move on to an easier target. According to the National Crime Prevention Institute, the average burglar takes no more than 60 seconds to break into a home. If you can delay his break-in 90 seconds or longer, he may get nervous and leave.

WHAT YOU CAN DO:

- Add deadbolt locks that extend at least 1½ inches into the door frame. Install a metal strike plate as well. This will make it more difficult for a burglar to kick in your door. (Most experts recommend either a deadbolt lock that requires a key or a pin tumbler cylinder lock. We suggest you check with a locksmith for the best recommendation.)

- Consider adding a second deadbolt with a double-key lock. You can use this lock as an added precaution when you're gone. A double-key lock makes it more difficult to get into the house as well as to get things out of the house. NOTE: Be wary of using double-key deadbolt locks while you're in the house. In case of fire, you'll have a difficult time getting out the door yourself.

- Take care with keys. Don't leave them under a doormat, in the mailbox or hanging from a nail outside your home. Thieves know all the places to look for keys. Also, don't leave your keys in your coat pocket when you check your coat or hang it in a public place. Don't leave your home key with a parking attendant, since he could easily have a duplicate made while you're gone. And never carry an identification tag on your key ring. If you lose your key and a burglar finds it, he'll know where you live and how to get in.

- If you have sliding patio doors, reinforce them with a locking metal rod that prevents the door from being opened. Another option is to nail a piece of wood in the door channel. However, this option limits your use of the door as well.

- If you have a pet door, make sure it's no more than 6 inches across. Burglars have been known to slip children through larger pet doors so they can unlock the door.

- Install extra window locks. The ordinary sash fastener offers virtually no resistance to a burglar. Windows need either a sash fastener that can be locked with a key or a key lock built into the bottom window bar. You can also use eye bolts to lock windows to the frame. However, be sure that whatever device you install can easily be opened from the inside in case of fire.

- In high-crime areas, consider installing steel security

shutters. They give you much the same protection as burglar bars without trapping you inside the house in case of fire. Security shutters can easily be opened from the inside.

- Install storm windows. They provide an extra deterrent in that they force a burglar to crack two panes of glass to get inside.

- Drill a hole in the track that holds your garage door and insert either a pin or a padlock to prevent the door from being raised.

- Don't leave ladders outside. They can easily be used by burglars to enter upstairs windows.

- Make sure you use all the safeguards you install. Some 40 percent of burglars get into homes without using any force at all!

6 INSTALL AN ALARM SYSTEM.

Home security systems range in sophistication from a simple unit that sounds an alarm, to a very elaborate system with a silent alarm linked to the police or security guards. These systems range in price from a few hundred dollars up to several thousand.

This may seem like a big investment, but the cost of a burglary could far outweigh the cost of an alarm system. Also, some insurers will give you a 5% to 15% discount off your homeowner's insurance for installing such a system. These discounts alone could pay for the system in a few years.

WHAT YOU CAN DO:

- No matter which alarm system you choose, place decals on your windows and a sign out front to warn burglars of its presence. The intent of alarms isn't necessarily to help apprehend burglars. Rather, the objective is to scare them away.

- Before you decide on an alarm system, talk to friends and neighbors who have alarm systems to determine the best one for your needs and budget.

- Don't be lulled into a false sense of security by any system. Even with a burglar alarm, you still need to maintain your vigil and take other steps to prevent a break-in. No alarm system is an end unto itself. It is simply one more precaution you can take.

- Make sure your house number is clearly visible on the curb, house and mailbox. This will make it easier for police and security guards to locate your house in the event of a burglary or other emergency.

7. MARK ALL VALUABLES WITH IDENTIFYING NUMBERS OR SYMBOLS.

Law enforcement agencies in most cities have programs to help you mark personal property with identifying numbers. One such program is called OPERATION I.D., a citizen's burglary prevention program for use in homes and businesses.

The program involves marking property with an identifying number as a means of discouraging burglary and theft. In communities where it has been properly implemented, OPERATION I.D. has shown dramatic results in its ability to reduce burglaries.

There are two parts to the program. First, mark your valuables with your driver's license number so that your property can be easily traced. Second, display a sticker which tells would-be burglars that your property has been marked.

Law enforcement agencies that participate in such programs usually have engraving tools you can borrow and warning decals for your windows. Call your local police or sheriff's department for more information.

WHAT YOU CAN DO:

- Use your driver's license number with your state's two-letter prefix to mark your property.
- Engrave the number on the property where it cannot easily be dismantled or removed—and where it can't easily be seen.
- Once you have marked your property, display a warn-

ing sign to that effect in your window. This will help deter some burglars.

- Possessions to mark include: TV sets, stereo equipment, radios, personal computers, tape recorders, guns, fishing rods and reels, vacuum cleaners, small kitchen appliances, typewriters, adding machines, dictating machines, answering machines, VCRs, cameras, camcorders, binoculars, lawn mowers, bicycles, outboard motors, golf clubs, hand tools, power tools, watches and clocks.

- After marking your property, make a list of your valuables and keep a copy of the list in a safe place. If you become the victim of a burglary, you'll be able to quickly describe to police the property that has been stolen.

- For added protection, photograph your property and keep the photos in a safe place, or record your possessions on videotape as you walk through your home verbally describing them. If possible, keep these photos or videotapes in a safe deposit box at the bank. They'll help in identifying your stolen property. They're also very useful when filing insurance claims if your property is stolen or destroyed.

- Make sure you have adequate homeowner's or renter's insurance to cover your valuables against theft. In spite of all our efforts, burglars hit more than 3 million homes in 1991—and stole more than $3.4 billion in property.

8. DON'T TRY TO DEFEND YOUR PROPERTY AT THE RISK OF PERSONAL SAFETY.

Your chances of encountering a burglar in your home are slim. Most burglars want to be long gone by the time you return. But what do you do if a burglar breaks in not knowing you're there? Or if you walk in and encounter a burglary in progress?

WHAT YOU CAN DO:

- Don't confront the burglar. And think twice before you pull a gun or other weapon. He may take it away from you. Or respond by pulling his own gun. You don't want to have a shoot-out, especially if other family members are present.

- Chances are, if you don't provoke the burglar, he won't harm you.

- Don't fight him unless you or a family member is attacked. In that event, fight back with any and every means you have available.

- If you come face to face with a burglar, try to stay as calm and in control as you possibly can. Remember, the first thing you want to do is get him to leave your house—which is probably foremost in his mind, as well.

- Try to remember as many details about the intruder as you possibly can—race, height, weight, hair color, eye color and how he's dressed.

- If possible, avoid meeting him at all. If you hear a

burglar in your home, don't go to investigate. If you can do so, shut and lock a door between you and the burglar. Phone police, then open a window and yell for help. If you have to, break the window. Do anything to attract attention to your house.

- If you wake up and discover a burglar in your room, pretend to be asleep until he's gone.
- If you see signs your home has been burglarized when you come home, leave the house at once. The thief may still be inside. Go to a neighbor's house and call the police. DO NOT TRY TO RE-ENTER THE HOUSE TO APPREHEND THE THIEF. WAIT FOR POLICE TO ARRIVE.

9 GET INVOLVED WITH YOUR NEIGHBORHOOD WATCH PROGRAM.

Preventing burglaries is hard to do alone. Everyone in the neighborhood has to be involved and aware of what is going on in the immediate vicinity of their homes. A neighborhood watch program is a good way to start.

A neighborhood watch is simply a program of neighbors watching out for each others' property. Many neighborhoods across the country have already initiated them. If your neighborhood doesn't have one, get it started today.

The program can be implemented by holding a block meeting to discuss the concept and develop a simple plan. Your local police agency will usually send a representative to speak to the group and explain the program in greater detail. Most police agencies also will provide signs to place along roads in your neighborhood to warn burglars of your watch program.

Each neighbor can effectively watch only one side of the homes on either side, the front of the home across the street and the back of the home in back. But if EVERY neighbor did this, every home on the block would have some degree of surveillance.

For the program to work effectively, each resident must take an active role in both security improvement and observation of activities on the block.

Essentially, you become a nosy neighbor. However, the intent is not to spy on your neighbor, but to spy on any suspicious people that show up on your neighbor's property.

WHAT YOU CAN DO:

- Make a diagram of your block with the name, address and phone number of each resident.

- If you see something suspicious at your neighbor's house, call and alert the residents. It may turn out to be totally innocent, in which case your neighbor will know what's going on. On the other hand, it may be a burglary in progress.

- If you see something suspicious and your neighbor isn't home, call the police and report it immediately. NOTE: Unless you perceive it to be an emergency, don't call 911. If you're just reporting suspicious activity, call police on the regular line (always keep this number by your phone, along with other emergency numbers).

- If you observe a burglary in progress, call 911 to report it. However, DO NOT TRY TO STOP THE BURGLARY. WAIT FOR THE POLICE TO ARRIVE. If you can do so without putting yourself in danger, try to notice as much about the suspects as possible, and get the license number and description of any vehicles involved. But do it only from a safe vantage point inside your home.

10. KNOW HOW TO IDENTIFY SUSPICIOUS ACTIVITIES AND HOW TO REPORT THEM.

It's impossible for the police to protect us without the help of concerned citizens. The police can't be everywhere at once, so they have to rely on citizens to call and report suspicious persons and activities.

Some people fail to call police simply because they aren't aware of what constitutes suspicious activities. Others don't call for fear of appearing to be a nosy neighbor. Still others don't call because they take it for granted that someone else has already called.

WHAT YOU CAN DO:

If you see anything suspicious in your neighborhood, call the police immediately. Don't worry about bothering the police or being embarrassed if your suspicions prove unfounded. Instead, think of what might happen if you didn't report it.

OBVIOUS SUSPICIOUS ACTIVITIES:

- Basically anything that seems even slightly out of place for the area or during the time of day it occurs may signal a criminal activity.
- A stranger entering a neighbor's house when it is unoccupied could be a burglar.
- Gunshots, screams, the very agitated barking of dogs—anything suggestive of a struggle or foul play should be reported immediately.

- Merchandise offered for sale at ridiculously low prices could be stolen property.
- Anyone removing accessories, gasoline or license plates from a neighbor's car could be a thief.
- Anyone peering into parked cars could be looking for a car to steal or valuables to take from the car.
- Persons entering or leaving a business at odd hours could indicate a burglary.
- The sound of glass breaking or loud explosive noises could indicate a burglary, vandalism or an accident.
- Persons loitering around schools, playgrounds, secluded areas or in the neighborhood could be sex offenders or drug dealers.
- Persons around the neighborhood who do not live there could be burglars or drug dealers.
- Apparent business transactions being conducted from a vehicle could indicate drug sales or stolen property sales.
- Persons being forced into a vehicle could indicate everything from kidnapping to robbery to drug transactions.
- Open or broken windows at the home of a neighbor who is away could possibly indicate a burglary has taken place or is in progress.

NOT-SO-OBVIOUS SUSPICIOUS ACTIVITIES:

- Any strangers in your neighborhood going from door to door should arouse a degree of suspicion. Even solicitors or salesmen. Watch their activities for awhile. If, after a few houses, they try a door to see if it's locked, or if they go around to the side or back of a house, they could be "casing" the home or committing a burglary. Such activity is even more suspicious if one person waits out front or if there is a car following a few houses away.

- Anyone waiting in front of a house when the owner is away is suspicious. The person might be a lookout for a burglary in progress.

- A stranger running down the street, especially if he's carrying something of value, should arouse suspicion.

- If you see anyone carrying property at an unusual hour or at an unusual place, you should be suspicious.

- If you see a person who's exhibiting unusual mental or physical symptoms, it could indicate he's under the influence of drugs or needs medical or psychiatric assistance.

- If you notice a lot of traffic to and from a residence that occurs daily or on a regular basis (particularly during late hours), it could indicate the presence of drug dealers, a vice operation or a "fence" operation where stolen goods are being bought or sold.

- Any vehicle moving slowly through the neighborhood (or around schools, parks and playgrounds) following a course that appears aimless or repetitive is suspicious. Occupants of the car could be casing a neighborhood, involved in drug activities or looking for someone to rob or victimize sexually.

- Parked vehicles occupied by one or more persons are particularly suspicious at an unusual hour of the day or night. They could be possible lookouts for a burglary, even if the occupants appear to be lovers.

- Property being loaded into a vehicle in the driveway of a house where the occupant is away is suspicious, even if the vehicle is marked with signs indicating a repair or delivery service. More and more professional thieves are marking their vehicles (particularly vans and pick-up trucks) to look like plumbers or heating and air conditioning service companies.

- Property being loaded onto a marked or unmarked moving van could be suspicious, especially if you know the occupants and were not aware of their intentions to move. Professionals have completely stripped homes of all their possessions using this technique.

- Abandoned vehicles in your neighborhood are suspicious in that they may be stolen cars.

HOW TO REPORT SUSPICIOUS ACTIVITIES:

- Obviously, the first thing to do is call the police. If you think a burglary is in progress or that someone's life is in danger, call 911. If you're just suspicious of something and want to have the police check it out, call the regular police line. That way, you won't tie up 911 lines for a non-emergency. But don't be afraid to call to report even the least suspicious activities. Your call could prevent a crime. Be sure to keep emergency numbers by your phone at all times.

- Be prepared to give police your name, address and the phone number from which you are calling. Try to give as accurate a description of the situation as possible. Try to give the exact location of the activity and as much description as possible of the suspects and/or vehicles involved.

- If you're observing the activities from a distance, it may not be possible to tell much about the suspects. But if you're close enough, try to note things like their height, weight, race, sex, clothing or any other characteristics that will help identify the suspects by police arriving on the scene.

- If possible, get the license number of any vehicles involved along with the make, model, year and color.

11 BE ALERT TO THE DANGERS OF RAPE IN YOUR HOME.

Burglaries aren't the only crimes committed at home. Nearly one-third of all reported rapes are committed in victims' homes. If you're a single woman or a married woman who is home alone part of the day or night, you should be particularly alert to the dangers of rape.

Many of the same precautions you take against burglary also apply to rape prevention in the home. They bear repeating here.

WHAT YOU CAN DO:

- Never allow a stranger into your home when you're alone, regardless of the reason or how dire the emergency is supposed to be. You can offer to make an emergency phone call—but do it through closed doors while the stranger waits outside.

- Never let repairmen or servicemen come into your home unless you have requested their presence and only after they have shown you convincing identification. If you have any doubts at all, don't let them in.

- Never open the door to strangers. Install a peephole and use it every time someone knocks on your door. If you don't see anyone, don't open the door to investigate. They could be crouched down out of view, ready to enter if given the chance.

- If strangers call or come to your door, don't ignore them hoping they'll go away. They might try a break-in if they think you aren't home. Talk to them through the closed door. Never tell them that you are alone.

- Make sure you have dependable deadbolts on your doors. Make sure all windows have double locks. Keep doors and windows locked at all times.

- If you come home and find signs of forced entry, don't go inside. Go to the nearest phone in a safe place and call the police.

OTHER THINGS YOU CAN DO:

- If you live in an apartment, avoid going to the laundry room by yourself, especially at night. And don't take out the garbage at night, especially if you have to go out to an alley.

- If you have a dog, don't walk it at night by yourself. Even if it's a big dog, you could still be placing yourself in great danger.

- If you're a single woman, don't put your name on mail boxes or in the phone book. If you have to have a listing, use only your first initial and last name.

- If you live alone, try to let a family member or trusted friend know your destination when you leave, what time you expect to be home, and what route you'll be taking.

- If you live alone, don't work in your yard or your garage at night.

- If you have a trusted friend you can check in with, make it a habit of doing so each time you come home.

PROTECTION IN AND AROUND YOUR CAR

As difficult as it is to protect our lives and property in the sanctity of our homes, being out on the streets requires double the diligence.

Not only do we have to worry about becoming one of the 50,000 people who die in traffic-related deaths, or one of the two million people injured in traffic accidents each year, we also have to guard against car theft (there's one every 19 seconds), rape (one every five minutes), robbery (one every 49 seconds), aggravated assault (one every 30 seconds) and murder (one every 22 minutes).

It's safe to say that every time we leave home, we are literally laying our lives on the line.

The suggestions that follow will not guarantee your safety while you're out in your car. But they could possibly lower your risk of becoming a victim of crime. And nowadays, that's about all you could hope to expect.

12 Check Out the Scene Before Getting in Your Car.

Before entering your car, look around inside and out for anything or anybody that looks suspicious— particularly at shopping centers and commercial parking garages where thieves can hide behind other vehicles in wait of a victim. (Some muggers have been known to hide under a car until the owner approaches, then either grab or slash the victim's leg, roll out from under the car and rob or assault the victim.)

Have your keys in your hand as you approach the car. And keep your mind on what you're doing. If you're daydreaming or preoccupied with something else, you won't be as alert as you should be. Unlock the door and get in your car as quickly as possible and immediately re-lock the door. If you have to put anything in the trunk, do it quickly. Be watchful for anyone approaching from any direction.

Try to avoid parking next to vans with double-side doors. Gangs have been known to wait in such vans and then jump out the side door to attack unwary victims. If you see a van parked next to you that wasn't there when you parked, return to the building and ask a security guard to accompany you to your car.

Rely on your instincts. If you see something the least bit suspicious, go back inside the shopping center or building and call police or security personnel. ALWAYS KNOW THE PHONE NUMBER OF POLICE OR SECURITY PERSONNEL. In an emergency, you might not have time to look up a number.

If you're confronted by a suspicious person and can't get back to the store or building, try to keep the car between yourself and the other person. If you can do so without making yourself vulnerable, get inside the car (even on the passenger side) where you have a degree of protection. Quickly lock the door. Once you're in the car, don't stop to ask or answer questions. Leave the scene as fast as safely possible. As soon as you're out of harm's way, call and report the suspicious person. Your call could possibly save someone else from becoming a victim.

If the person exhibits threatening actions before you can get in your car, scream for help. If you have a car alarm, bump the car to activate the alarm. If you have a car alarm with a panic button, use it! At this point, do anything you can to attract the attention of others, all the while trying to keep the car between yourself and the mugger. If you're able to get inside your car, lock the doors immediately and leave the scene. Report the incident to police or security as soon as possible.

If the person pulls a gun and threatens you, comply with his demands up to a point. It may be that all he wants is your car or purse, and it's probably safer not to offer resistance. Your life is far more important than your car, wallet or jewelry. However, you should still try to keep the car as a buffer between yourself and the mugger. Try to comply with his demands by tossing items across the car to him.

If the mugger takes your keys and demands that you get in the car, the situation has changed dramatically. Once the mugger gets you in the car and away from the scene, rape or murder could be the consequence. Some crime prevention experts advise that you should do everything possible to avoid being abducted. This may involve screaming, fighting, begging, pleading or running away. It's a critical decision to have to make in a split second. No one can say for certain how to best handle this situation. The best advice we could hope to give is this: stay alert and be extremely wary of the slightest suspicious activity. That way, you might avoid ever having to make this life or death decision.

WHAT YOU CAN DO:

- Stay alert and keep your mind on what you're doing.
- Have your keys in hand, ready to unlock the door.
- Check out the scene around your car for anything suspicious.
- If something seems suspicious, go to a safe place and report it.
- Look inside your car before getting in to make sure no one is hiding inside.
- Make it a point to lock all car doors as soon as you get in your car—every time, without exception, even if you're just going a few blocks down the street. It should become as much a part of your routine as buckling your seat belt.
- Never leave your unattended car running while you run inside a home or business "for just a minute".
- Never leave your keys in your car.
- Never leave your car doors unlocked when you park.

50 WAYS TO PROTECT YOURSELF AGAINST CRIME.

- Never leave your windows down when you park.
- Never try to approach your vehicle if anything looks the least bit suspicious.
- Never park your car in dark, unlighted parking lots.

13 KNOW WHERE YOU'RE GOING BEFORE YOU LEAVE.

This sounds pretty elementary. But a lot of people set out for a location knowing "about where it is" and only vaguely how to get there. This is especially true of people out of town on business or pleasure. But it's also a fairly common occurrence while right in your own town. Let's say you're going to meet some friends in an "out of the way" restaurant. You know generally where it's located, but it's situated in a part of town where you rarely go. You leave for the restaurant without knowing specifically how to get there or the safest route to take. What happens if you take a wrong turn? Or if you get lost along the way and end up in a high-crime neighborhood? You could be placing your property and personal safety in great danger.

Before you leave to go anywhere, get the specific address of your destination. If you have any doubts about how to get there, look at a road map. But don't rely on a map alone. A map may show you the shortest route, but not the safest. Ask the advice of someone who's familiar with the area, the most obvious being someone who lives or works at the destination itself. If it's in a part of town you're unfamiliar with, inquire about the safest route to take.

Even if you have to go a little out of your way, it's better to be safe than punctual. Shortcuts that take you through unfamiliar, lightly traveled areas can make you more vulnerable to crime. Every time you stop for a red light or stop sign, you're at greater risk if nobody else is around. What if you accidentally ended up on a dead-end street? There's only one way out, and you've got to turn around to get to it. Your path could easily be blocked by another vehicle. At that point, you and your property might be at the mercy of criminals. And criminals show little mercy to either.

The onslaught of gang activity and drug dealing has turned even innocent-looking neighborhoods into war zones. So your best bet is to avoid unfamiliar areas altogether.

WHAT YOU CAN DO:

- Know the specific address of your destination.
- Know the safest route to your destination.
- Allow yourself ample time to reach your destination without rushing. When you're rushed, you're distracted; when you're distracted, you're vulnerable.
- Never take shortcuts through unfamiliar areas.
- Never travel along dark, lightly traveled streets.
- Never go down any street if there's the slightest sign of danger.

14. TELL A FRIEND OR RELATIVE WHERE YOU'RE GOING AND WHEN YOU'LL RETURN.

Remember the "buddy system" we used as kids? This idea is much the same. If we're lost or missing, there'll be somebody to alert the authorities. It may sound childish to suggest that we need someone to know our whereabouts as adults. But in an age when a violent crime occurs every 17 seconds, it's a good plan to follow.

Every time we leave our homes, we run the risk of becoming a victim of crime (sometimes we're victimized right in the sanctity of our homes). Something as simple as going to the corner store for a loaf of bread can lead to a life threatening situation. The same is true when we go to work, to a party, to school or any place outside the home.

We're not suggesting that you tell someone every time you set foot out your door. And we're not trying to create mass hysteria. But if you really want to play it safe, it's important that someone know where you are and when you're supposed to return. That way, if you don't arrive at your destination at a designated time, there'll be somebody to either alert the police or come looking for you. If you were actually having trouble, you'd welcome someone trying to help.

To avoid false alarms or needless worry, establish an absolute deadline for reaching your destination. For example, you're supposed to be back at your apartment by midnight. So you tell your roommate if you're not back by at least 1:00, alert someone to come looking for you. If you have a change in plans and know you'll be late, call and let your buddy know.

It's also a good idea to tell your buddy what route you'll be taking so they'll know where to start looking for you.

Make sure your buddy is someone you know and trust, preferably a relative or roommate. You certainly don't want to give such information to someone you don't know very well.

WHAT YOU CAN DO:

- Tell a buddy where you're going and when you'll return.
- Tell a buddy what route you'll be taking.
- Call and tell of any change in plans or routes.
- Never deviate from your plans without telling your buddy.
- Never choose a buddy you don't know and trust.

15. PLAN YOUR TRIPS FOR THE DAYLIGHT HOURS WHENEVER POSSIBLE.

We have good reason to be afraid of the dark. More than 58% of violent crimes occur during the hours of darkness. Criminals seem to live for the night when the roads are less traveled, the streets are emptier and shadowy hiding places are plentiful.

In many cases, we can't avoid being out after dark. A lot of entertainment activities are scheduled for the evening hours, and if we're to enjoy them, we have no choice but to be out at night. Activities involving young children (baseball, soccer, football, school plays, etc.) should always include adult supervision. Children should never be allowed to be out alone after dark—even to walk a couple of blocks from a park to home.

Whenever possible, try to re-schedule nighttime activities for the daylight hours. Many families where both parents work (or a single parent) do their shopping in the evening after work. Try to do as much shopping as possible on weekends or in the early evening hours before dark. Mail order shopping is another alternative. But be cautious here as well. Make sure the mail order firm is stable and reputable. You don't want to be victimized by mail fraud or credit card fraud.

If you have errands to run, try to get them done in the afternoon or early evening before it's completely dark. But a word of caution. Don't be lulled into a false sense of security in the daylight hours. If you lower your guard, you can easily be victimized in broad daylight. "Stay alert, stay alive" are words to live by around the clock.

WHAT YOU CAN DO:

- Try to do your shopping during the daylight hours.
- If you have to be out after dark, try to have another person with you.
- Be extremely alert and wary of suspicious people or situations.
- Never allow young children to be out alone after dark for any reason.

16 AVOID CONFRONTATIONS WITH OTHER MOTORISTS.

The crime wave sweeping across America has alarmed citizens to the point that many are now carrying guns to protect their lives and property. Although carrying a handgun either on your person or in your car is illegal in most states, it has become fairly commonplace for motorists to carry them in their vehicles.

A handgun carried for defense can just as easily become an offensive weapon in the heat of an argument or a confrontation between motorists in traffic. In recent years, the incidence of a driver pulling a gun and firing at another motorist has become too common for comfort.

Bearing in mind that many motorists are armed (and possibly dangerous), it's best to avoid any confrontation no matter how slight. If you do something to provoke the anger of another driver, don't aggravate the situation further with gestures, words or glares. Try to avoid making eye contact with the other motorist, and as soon as safely possible, turn onto another street or roadway away from the angry driver. It won't serve any purpose whatsoever if you turn the incident into a test of will or strength. You haven't lost anything by avoiding a conflict. You've possibly saved your life.

Something else to consider before you take issue with another motorist: some people who are out there driving have also been drinking. Do you really want to deal with a potential drunk in a car with a gun?

Your best defense? Stay calm and in control. Drive courteously. Obey traffic laws. And don't let your emotions get in the way of common sense.

WHAT YOU CAN DO:

- Drive courteously and obey traffic laws.
- Remember that many motorists carry guns.
- Remember that some motorists have been drinking and that alcohol is a depressant that can heighten anger and aggression.
- Stay calm and in control of the situation.
- Never turn an encounter in traffic into a test of will or a matter of principle.
- Never shout or gesture angrily at another motorist.
- Never stop your car and get out to encounter another motorist.

17 BE AS INCONSPICUOUS AS POSSIBLE.

In the summer of 1991, in Houston, Texas, the wife of a prominent rock band manager was abducted and murdered. Her abduction took place in the middle of the day as she stopped at a pay phone near her home in a "respectable", low-crime area.

A few days later, a suspect was captured (a parolee less than 24 hours out of the penitentiary). He confessed to her murder and told police that her red Cadillac had initially caught his attention as he loitered in the vicinity of the pay phone. He said he had also noticed her expensive clothes and jewelry. It was easy to see she was a wealthy woman. Sadly, now she's dead.

Her case was no isolated incident. A few months earlier, a Houston woman in a red sports car was brutally murdered while waiting at the drive-through window at a fast-food restaurant. It was 2:00 in the afternoon. The killer wanted her car.

A few months later a prominent Houston businessman was killed in the driveway of his fashionable home at 10:00 PM. The killer had followed him home from an expensive restaurant.

The list goes on and on. Another wealthy Houstonian, murdered at a car wash beside his expensive sports car at 10:30 at night. A Penthouse model in a cocktail dress murdered outside a convenience store at 3:00 in the morning as she waited in her girlfriend's custom Mercedez while her girlfriend talked on a pay phone.

It's perfectly normal to want to enjoy your possessions. Unfortunately, though, a show of wealth or affluence can easily mark you for crime.

If you drive an expensive car, be especially watchful for anyone who might be following you. This is particularly true when leaving restaurants or shopping areas. For some reason, bright red cars seem to attract the most attention. So if your car is both expensive and red, be extra alert. If you think someone is following you, don't lead them to your home. Go to a pre-determined safe place and call the police. Otherwise, you could either be attacked when you get out of your car, or the thieves might come back at a later time to burglarize your home.

Also, be selective about when and where you wear expensive-looking jewelry. And exercise great caution when you do. Thieves are looking for something that's easy to sell. Jewelry fits the bill nicely. It's also a tip-off that you may be affluent. If you have nice jewelry, chances are good that you have a houseful of other nice things that any thief would love. Here again, when you go out wearing expensive jewelry, keep an eye out for anyone following you. Remember, don't go home if you're being followed. Instead, go to a pre-determined safe place and call the police.

If you're like most people, you're probably driving the most expensive car you can afford. But a less expensive-looking car is something to consider. You might also want to give a little more thought to the color of your next car and some of the exterior frills that make it stand out in the crowd. That's the last thing you want to do these days.

Another thing to consider is tinted windows. Dark-tinted windows make it difficult for thieves to see inside your car, which means they can't tell how many people are in the car or what's inside. A word of caution though. Many states have laws that govern how dark car windows can be. Make sure your tinting complies with the law.

None of the foregoing is meant to imply that thieves only take note of expensive cars. The fact is, most cars are stolen by amateurs. If you make it easy for them, they'll steal just about any car that moves, from the flashiest to the plainest.

WHAT YOU CAN DO:

- Try to be as low-key as possible in the way you dress and the jewelry you wear.

- Be extremely alert when wearing expensive jewelry.

- Be extremely alert when leaving shopping areas and expensive restaurants.

- Know the location of safe places you can go in the event of trouble. The safest place would be a police station. Other safe places might include fire stations, all-night supermarkets with a security guard, apartment complexes with security guards and all-night restaurants.

- Never drive home if you think you're being followed. Go to a safe place and call the police.

- Never keep your house key on a key chain you leave with a parking attendant, and never tell a parking attendant how long you'll be gone if you don't have to.

- Unless it's an absolute emergency, never stop at pay phones where you're visible from the street when you're wearing expensive jewelry or clothing (or any other time if you can avoid it).

18 MAKE YOUR CAR HARD TO STEAL.

More than a million cars are stolen in the U.S. each year, and literally millions of others are stripped or vandalized. Most of these cars were easy prey because their owners didn't take a few simple precautions that make it hard on thieves. True, you can't make your car impossible to steal; a professional thief can usually get it in spite of your best efforts. But the fact is, most cars are stolen by amateurs, not professionals. So it will definitely pay to take a few extra precautions.

WHAT YOU CAN DO:

- Lock your car with the windows rolled up tightly every time you leave it (even for a few minutes). Eighty percent of all the cars stolen are unlocked at the time. A window that's even slightly open makes your car more vulnerable.

- NEVER leave the keys in the ignition. Believe it or not, 40% of all stolen cars had the keys in the ignition.

- No matter how short the errand, don't leave your motor running. A lot of amateur thieves hang out around convenience stores and pay phones waiting for a careless motorist to come along.

- If you use valet parking, make certain the attendant actually works for the parking lot. Amateur thieves sometimes pose as valet parking attendants and simply drive off with your car after you hand them the keys.

- Carry spare keys in your purse or wallet. Don't hide keys under the hood or anywhere else on or in the car. Most thieves know all the hiding places.

- When you park your car in the driveway, back in with the engine facing the street so anyone tampering with the engine can easily be seen. If your home has a garage, park your car inside it and lock both your car and garage.

- Whether parking your car in your driveway or on the street, turn the steering wheel sharply to the left or right before turning off the ignition which engages the column lock. This makes your car harder to tow which is a ploy of some professionals.

- Try to find a spot that's well lighted and heavily trafficked if you have to park on the street.

- Never give parking attendants any key but the ignition key.

Remember, the more difficult you make it for a thief, the less likely you are to have your car stolen. The precautions outlined above won't cost a dime and take almost no extra effort at all. In the section immediately following, you'll find additional protective measures that require a modest investment of time or money.

19 MAKE YOUR CAR EVEN HARDER TO STEAL.

In 1990, a car was stolen every nineteen seconds in America, creating a billion dollar criminal industry. Although professionals increasingly enter the field, making it more and more difficult to protect your car, there are a number of devices on the market that greatly impede auto theft. These anti-theft devices cost anywhere from a few dollars to several hundred dollars. If you're serious about protecting your car, they're worth considering. None of them are foolproof, but they can at least slow down even accomplished professionals. The longer it takes to steal your car, the more likely it is to attract attention and prevent the theft from occurring.

ANTI-THEFT DEVICES:

- TAPERED DOOR LOCKS—These slim tapered interior door locks can be used to replace conventional door locks. They're almost impossible to pull up with a clothes hanger.

- KILL SWITCH—Prevents the car from being started unless a hidden switch is activated.

- ALARM SYSTEMS—A device that activates a siren, lights or horn if the car is tampered with. (Keys or code numbers should never be given out to a parking attendant.)

- FUEL SWITCH—A hidden switch that cuts off the fuel supply.

- STEERING COLUMN LOCKING DEVICES—There are a number of systems that rely on either metal bars or metal collars to lock the steering wheel in place so that it can't be turned.

- KEYLESS ENTRY SYSTEM—This system uses a remote control device with either a switch or button code to unlock and lock the car door.

- SEPARATE LOCKS—This involves installing separate locks for the door, ignition and trunk. That way, if a thief should get the key to your car door, at least he won't have an ignition key to get the car started. And if you have valuables in your trunk, they'll be harder to steal.

WHAT YOU CAN DO:

- If you go out of town and leave your car at home or in a parking lot, remove the distributor cap or coil wire so it can't be started.

- Mount CB radios, tape decks and telephones out of sight. If possible, take them with you or lock them in the trunk.

- Engrave your vehicle identification number on all window glass, trim, door frames, bumpers and accessories. Marked parts are easier to trace and are more difficult for thieves to sell.

- Engrave your vehicle identification number on any accessories that can be removed from the car (stereos, CB radios, phones, T-tops, wheel covers, tire rims, spare tires, etc.).

- Unless required by state law, don't keep your title or registration in your car. That just makes it easier for the thief to sell your car if it's stolen.

NOTE: Some insurance companies give a discount for certain anti-theft devices and for vehicles with engraved identifying marks.

20 DON'T LEAVE AN OPEN INVITATION IN YOUR CAR.

Packages, purses, wallets, or checkbooks left on the seat of your car are very enticing to thieves. Even stereo tapes and loose change. If a thief can see them in your car, it's like an open invitation to come take them, particularly if your car is unlocked or parked in a remote, unsecured area.

Portable car phones are particularly enticing. Since they can be operated off the power of any car's cigarette lighter, a thief can use a stolen car phone for weeks in his own car before the calls can be traced. Usually, calls from stolen phones are made for illegal activities that are even more difficult to trace.

WHAT YOU CAN DO:

- When shopping, lock all packages out of sight in the trunk. If a thief can't see them, he's less likely to break into your car.

- When you exit the car, take your purse or wallet with you. If you leave either in view inside your car even briefly, you're inviting a thief to come and take them. Many will gladly accept your invitation.

- If possible, lock car phones, stereos, CB radios and the like in the trunk. If any such equipment has a portable antenna, lock that in the trunk as well.

- Roll the windows up snugly and lock your car doors. This should become a part of your routine every time you park your car.

- Never leave infants or children unattended in a parked vehicle—even for an instant! They're extremely vulnerable to child molesters and kidnappers. There have even been cases where thieves have stolen cars not knowing that an infant was sleeping in the back seat.
- Never leave anything of value in open view.
- Never leave checkbooks or bank statements in open view. Even your account number can be used by slick criminals to fraudulently get money from your account.

21 KNOW WHAT TO DO IF YOUR CAR BREAKS DOWN.

Hopefully, your car will never give you any trouble. Of course, that's hoping for a lot. Cars are imperfect machines to begin with. And machines break down. Add the daily rigors of high-speed freeway driving, rush-hour traffic, pot holes and speed bumps, and the odds are good that your car will break down at some point in time.

Once was, if you had car trouble on the road, you could flag down a passing motorist and go for help. Those days appear to be gone forever. If you get in the car with a stranger, you may be gone forever as well.

WHAT YOU CAN DO:

- The first thing to do if your car has a mechanical failure is to try to maneuver it safely to the edge of the roadway out of the path of other traffic. Turn on your emergency flashers.

- If the car is still operable, say in the case of a flat tire, continue to drive the car slowly along the side of the roadway until you reach a safe, well-lighted place where you can get help. You may ruin the tire in the process. But the tire is replaceable.

- Don't get out of the car and try to change the tire or make other repairs! If you have roadway flares, position them conspicuously by your vehicle. Get back inside the car as quickly as possible and make sure all doors are locked. Place a "Call Police" sign in your rear window and remain in your car until police arrive.

- If you can get to a roadside telephone or call-box safely, do so. If not, STAY IN THE CAR WITH THE DOORS LOCKED.

- If you have a car phone, call for help. (Nowadays, a car phone is one of the best pieces of emergency equipment you can have in your car.)

- If you have to use a CB radio, be extremely wary. Your broadcast could just as easily attract criminals as it could good samaritans.

- If someone stops to offer assistance, stay in your locked car and ask the person to get help. Crack the window just enough to allow you to talk to the person offering help. DON'T OPEN YOUR CAR DOOR. DON'T LEAVE WITH A STRANGER!

- If no one stops to offer help, remain in the vehicle until a police car or wrecker comes by. (If you use the "buddy system" discussed in item 14 above, someone will know to come looking for you.)

- Always try to have an emergency plan for car failure.

- Carry proper safety and emergency equipment in your car. (If you can possibly afford a car phone, get one.)

- Always carry emergency phone numbers in your car.

- Try to know the exact location of safe places you can drive to.

- Travel well-lighted, busy streets whenever possible.

- Never take shortcuts through isolated, unfamiliar parts of town.

- Never stop to render aid to a stranded motorist if you have to get out of your car to do so (unless, of course, it's the result of a car accident where someone has been seriously hurt, in which case, you'll have to use your best judgement and follow your instincts). In many cases, the safest way to render assistance is to proceed immediately to a safe place and call the police.

22 GUARD AGAINST CAR-JACKING.

When you stop at intersections, you're vulnerable to a hijacker jumping in your car and either forcing you out, or worse yet, taking you with him. A crime like this was virtually unheard of a few years ago. Today, it's becoming more and more commonplace in big cities. And it often occurs in broad daylight, at the height of rush-hour traffic!

WHAT YOU CAN DO:

- Roll your windows up and lock all doors when you're driving. If you need the windows open, crack them slightly but not enough for someone to reach inside.

- Keep your purse and other valuables out of sight while you're driving. If a thief can't see it, he may not be as tempted.

- If someone does try to open your car door for any reason, don't stop to ask questions. Drive away quickly but safely. Try not to panic and cause a traffic accident.

- If someone approaches your car to ask for directions or assistance, don't roll down your window all the way. Crack it just enough to communicate.

- When you pull up to a stop sign or red light, keep your car in gear.

- Try to leave at least one full car length between your car and the car in front of you. That way, you won't be trapped without an escape route. If you see someone suspicious approaching your car, you'll at least have room to maneuver and drive away if you feel threatened. Try not to panic though. Make sure the way is clear before you pull over into another lane of traffic. Otherwise, you could be injured or killed in a collision.

- If another car bumps you from the rear, your first inclination is to get out and check the damage. Be extremely cautious before you do! Look in your rearview mirror. Is the driver of the car that bumped you getting out of the car or is it one of the passengers? If it's a passenger instead of the driver, the passenger could easily jump in your car and drive away while you're surveying the damage done to your car. If you feel the least bit suspicious, drive to a safe place, then get out and survey the damage. Report the incident to police. Report the damages to your insurance company. A WORD OF CAUTION: Don't leave the scene of an accident if it's serious or if an injury is involved. You could be charged with leaving the scene of an accident. If you have to remain at the scene, stay in your locked car if possible. However, if you can see that an injury is involved, you should render aid and call for help.

23. KNOW THE LOCATION OF "SAFE PLACES".

Safe places are locations where you can find a degree of protection when you feel threatened. These include police stations, fire stations, all-night drug stores, supermarkets, convenience stores and apartment complexes with security guards. Obviously, some places are safer than others, and you should choose the one that takes you out of immediate danger the quickest.

SOME SAFE PLACES TO KNOW:

- POLICE STATIONS are probably the safest places to go. They are usually manned 24 hours a day with armed law enforcement officers whose job is to protect you. However, some police stations are situated in high-crime neighborhoods, so it's important to know exactly where various police stations are and how to reach them with the least amount of risk. There have actually been cases of people being robbed or murdered right outside police stations, so just because you're able to drive there doesn't necessarily guarantee your safety. If you're being pursued by criminals and you manage to reach a police station, you may be better off staying in your car and honking your horn to alert the officers inside. It all depends on the situation and the risk involved in leaving your car and trying to get inside the station.

- FIRE STATIONS offer the safety of numbers. They usually have three or more firefighters on duty around the clock. While these people aren't peace officers, and as a rule aren't armed, they are trained to deal with emergencies, and they usually have direct communications to summon police. It's important to know the exact location of fire stations near the route you travel. If you get lost while trying to reach a safe place, you may be placing yourself in even greater danger.

- ALL-NIGHT SUPERMARKETS AND DRUG STORES are public places usually frequented by a number of people day and night. In the evening hours, many of these stores have armed security guards on the premises. Here again, it's important to know the exact location of these places.

- LARGE APARTMENT COMPLEXES often have security guards on duty to protect the property of the residents. However, since these guards are generally patrolling the apartment grounds, you may not be able to locate them once you've arrived. If that's the case, lean on your horn to alert either security guards or residents.

- CONVENIENCE STORES probably offer the least safety of all. There's usually only one clerk on duty who may or may not be armed. Also, convenience stores themselves are often the targets of armed robbers. Go to convenience stores only if you can't reach another safe place.

WHAT YOU CAN DO:

- Make a list of safe places, complete with the address and directions, and keep it in your car.

- Try to know in advance exactly which safe place you'd choose from different points along your route.
- Write down emergency phone numbers and keep the list in your car (along with small change for pay phones).
- Never get out of your car, even at a safe place, if a criminal is blocking your way. (Stay in the car and lean on the horn to alert the people inside.)
- Never worry about being embarrassed by false alarms. If you feel threatened, follow your instincts and proceed to a safe place.
- Never try to reach a safe place that's in an unfamiliar location unless you feel extremely threatened. If you get lost or take a wrong turn, you could end up in even greater danger.

24 DON'T TAKE UNNECESSARY RISKS.

To some degree, everything in life is a risk. The simple act of walking out your front door is risky. Driving an automobile certainly qualifies as a high-risk activity. Not only are you exposed to the possibility of injury or death from a traffic accident, you also run the risk of being victimized by criminals. One way to protect yourself from either eventuality is to minimize the risks you take.

WHAT YOU CAN DO WHEN DRIVING:

- Never pick up a hitchhiker! No matter how innocent or "clean-cut" a person may look, he or she could still be dangerous.

- Don't drive strangers home from parties or clubs. You're playing Russian roulette every time you allow a stranger into your car for any reason.

- Don't go to Automatic Teller Machines at night, especially if they're not well lit or if they're located in secluded areas. Don't use any Automatic Teller Machine, night or day, if suspicious-looking people are nearby.

- When conducting business at a bank's drive-through window, always keep your doors locked and your windows rolled up. Roll your window down only when it's your turn. Be on the lookout for suspicious persons on foot or suspicious vehicles. If anyone suspicious approaches your vehicle, leave immediately. You can always come back.

- Don't stop and use pay phones along roadways, particularly at night. Thieves and robbers sometimes wait near pay phones and watch for potential victims.

- If at all possible, avoid driving on dark, unlighted streets in unfamiliar parts of town.

- When you get home, leave your headlights on until you have the car in the garage and the house door unlocked. If your garage has a remote-control garage door opener, get in the habit of using it. That way, you can stay in your locked car until you've closed and locked the garage door behind you.

- If you carry large amounts of cash, don't tell anyone. And don't flash it around. If possible, carry only emergency cash with you.

- Be particularly alert when leaving a bank or other business establishment where people get cash or other items of value.

WHAT YOU CAN DO AS A PEDESTRIAN:

To say "it isn't safe to walk the streets any more" is an understatement to say the least. As vulnerable as you are in your car, it pales in comparison to the dangers you face as a pedestrian. Many victims are people simply out for an evening stroll or walking home from a bus stop. If you have to walk somewhere, be extremely cautious and don't take risks.

- Never hitchhike or accept rides from strangers!
- Avoid walking alone at night. If you live in a high-crime area, avoid walking at night period.
- Avoid walking on dimly lit streets or through alleys and tunnels. Never take shortcuts through lightly-traveled areas. Stay in well-lighted areas as much as possible.
- Walk on the part of the sidewalk closest to the street, as far away as possible from shrubs, trees and doorways. You may even be safer walking in the street than on the sidewalk.
- Walk confidently, directly and at a steady pace. Walk on the side of the street facing oncoming traffic.
- Wear clothes and shoes that give you freedom of movement.
- If someone drops you off alone, have them wait until you are in the house before they drive away.
- Stay out of public parks at night.
- If you're in trouble, attract attention any way you can. Scream, yell "Fire!", or break a window in a house where you think someone is home.
- Be careful if someone stops you and asks for directions. Always reply from a safe distance. Never get too close to the car.
- Just because you're walking in your neighborhood or an area that's familiar to you, don't drop your guard. Be cautious all the time.
- Carry your purse upside down with your hand on the clasp. If someone tries to grab your purse, open the

clasp and spill the contents out (this will force the thief to rummage through your valuables on the ground to find what he wants, and the time this requires might deter him). If you are physically able to run and believe you can safely get away from the scene, run to safety as fast as you can. If you're in no condition to run, immediately sit down to reduce your chances of being knocked down and injured.

25 ALWAYS BE PREPARED FOR AN EMERGENCY.

As we discussed in items 18, 19 and 20, there are numerous means available to help protect your car and the property inside. But what about your personal protection?

You could carry a weapon, but most law enforcement officials discourage it. Remember, in most states, it's against the law to carry a hand gun on your person or in your car in most circumstances.

Furthermore, without proper training and extreme safety measures, guns can be very dangerous to have around—especially if you have children. There's even the possibility that your gun will be stolen and used to commit a crime, or even worse, used against you.

Before you decide to carry a gun, we strongly urge you to check with law enforcement officials in your area regarding laws and procedures.

Short of carrying a gun, there are other steps you can take to increase your personal security while driving.

WHAT YOU CAN DO:

- If you can work it into your budget, get a car phone. Prices of car telephones have finally reached a level that makes them affordable for large numbers of people. Several reliable brands sell for under $50. Transportable phones that plug into the car's cigarette lighter can be transferred from one car to another. And many cellular phone companies have special rates for limited use. If you purchase a car phone strictly for security and limit its use to emergencies only, monthly charges can be held to a minimum. Should you have car trouble or some other emergency while you're on the road, a car phone allows you to remain in your car and phone for help. Some cellular phone companies even provide special emergency roadside assistance numbers. (You might even want to consider a small, portable cellular phone that fits in your purse or coat pocket. Since these phones are battery operated, you can call for help while you're walking to and from your car.)

- Another inexpensive item worth considering is the service of an automobile club or association that provides 24-hour towing and roadside assistance. Most of these associations promise to provide assistance within an hour after your call. This service, combined with a car phone, can help increase your safety and peace of mind when you have to be out in your car, especially at night.

- Always keep a flashlight with fresh batteries inside your car. It'll come in handy if you have car trouble at night.

- Have a fold-up sign with a "Call Police" message.

- It's also a good idea to keep a road map in the glove compartment with safe places marked.

- Be sure to keep emergency phone numbers in a handy place inside the vehicle.

- Place four quarters in an envelope along with a list of emergency phone numbers. If your car breaks down on the road, and a stranger stops to offer help, crack your window just enough to pass the envelope through. This procedure will make it easier for someone to get help while you remain inside your locked car.

PRECAUTIONS TO TAKE WHILE TRAVELING

Thieves are always trying to catch you with your guard down. And what better time than when you're on vacation, enjoying your leisure time?

You're supposed to relax and get away from it all. Unfortunately, there seems to be no getting away from crime. It's with you wherever you go.

During the summer months and around the holidays, when many honest citizens look for a little rest and relaxation, criminals seem to work their hardest. Therefore, it's imperative that you realize the many ways you can be victimized by crime.

The following suggestions will serve to make you more aware of your vulnerability and help you develop preventive measures to reduce the risk of being victimized.

26 DON'T LET YOUR CAR GIVE AWAY THE FACT THAT YOU'RE A TOURIST.

When you go traveling, crime can become an unpleasant part of your trip unless you take extra precautions. During the summer months and around the holidays, criminals seem to work even harder to separate you from your possessions.

Thieves often victimize vacationers' cars because they know that's where possessions are kept. Thieves love cameras, camcorders, clothing and cash that most tourists carry with them. And a lot of times, they can see valuables because they're left out in plain sight inside the car.

WHAT YOU CAN DO:

- Don't leave clothing hanging in a car where thieves can "window shop".

- Don't leave luggage out in plain sight in your car. A thief thinks that's an open invitation to take what belongs to you. Your spare clothing and luggage are safer in the trunk (even though it only takes a thief a short time to break into the trunk).

- Don't leave maps and travel brochures laying on the dash or in seats. These are telltale signs that you're on vacation.

- Never leave a camera, purse or wallet in your car when it's unattended—even for a few minutes. These items are too tempting for a thief to pass up.

- Lock your possessions in your trunk when you stop at restaurants or scenic points along the way.
- Remember, your out-of-state license plates are a dead giveaway that you're an "out-of-towner". Be extra cautious with your possessions.
- Keep your possessions out of view in your car as much as possible—even while you're driving.
- Never leave packages or presents in view in your car. Around the holidays, thieves are extremely active.

27 UNLOAD YOUR CAR WHEN YOU STOP EACH NIGHT.

Parking lots at motels are places thieves routinely monitor. If you're careless with your possessions, they could easily be gone the next morning.

Thieves know that tourists, being tired from a long drive, often leave valuables in their car overnight. The best way to keep your possessions from being stolen is to keep them with you—either in your hotel room or locked in the hotel safe.

WHAT YOU CAN DO:

- As troublesome as it may seem, you should make it a point to unload your car when you stop for the night.

- Roadside motels where cars are left unattended during the night are particularly vulnerable.

- If possible, park near your room within earshot of car tampering.

- If your car has an alarm, don't forget to activate it.

- If you're pulling a trailer loaded with the kind of belongings you can't unload overnight, you're particularly vulnerable. Make sure the trailer has a strong padlock, and keep it locked at all times. If at all possible, put an alarm on the trailer. Try to park in a well-lit area as close to your room as possible. If you can't park close to your room, try to park near the office where an attendant is on duty. If possible, back the trailer all the way to a wall or close enough to a wall to prevent the trailer door from being opened and the contents being removed.

- Never leave anything of value in your car at hotels where you have to leave the car key with a parking attendant (make sure you leave only the ignition key). If you read the fine print on the back of most claim checks, you'll notice that the hotel disclaims all responsibility for anything you leave in your car. There's good reason for such disclaimers.

28. AT AIRPORTS, TAKE SPECIAL PRECAUTIONS WITH PURSES AND LUGGAGE.

Airports are fraught with perils for your purse, luggage and cameras. Thieves routinely work airports waiting for someone to leave luggage or possessions unattended. They arouse no suspicion at all in picking up unattended luggage and walking out with it.

WHAT YOU CAN DO:

- Be particularly careful with your possessions in the following airport areas:

AT CURBSIDE PASSENGER DROP-OFF POINTS. When you arrive at the airport, usually the first thing you do is set your bags on the curb and then hail a skycap to help with your bags. During peak hours, however, skycaps aren't always readily available. Stay with your bags until a skycap is available. Either that or carry your bags yourself. Never leave your bags unattended while you go looking for a skycap.

WHILE WAITING IN CHECK-IN LINES. It's not uncommon for people to leave their carry-on luggage in a waiting room seat while they stand in the check-in line. After all, luggage is heavy and cumbersome and it's tiresome having to lug it around. If you let down your guard, however, you may be left without your bags. Keep them with you in the check-in line unless you're traveling with a companion who can watch them for you.

IN RESTROOMS. In most airport restrooms, it's physically impossible to keep your luggage in view while you use the facilities. Most stalls aren't large enough to accommodate both you and your luggage.

If you don't have a companion who can watch your bags, rent a locker and store your bags. Never set bags down outside a stall, or even worse, outside the restroom. It only takes an instant for a thief to make off with them.

IN RESTAURANTS AND SNACK BARS. Here again, there is a tendency for some travelers to go into a restaurant, set their bags at a table, then leave them while they go to the counter to order food or go through a buffet line.

Even though it's troublesome, keep your bags with you unless you have a companion who can wait at the table with the bags while you order the food.

AT SECURITY CHECKPOINTS. When you go through security checkpoints at airports, KEEP YOUR EYES ON YOUR PURSE AT ALL TIMES. You will lose sight of it briefly as it goes through the X-ray unit, but try to be there waiting when it comes through. If you get stopped at the metal detector walkway, ask the guard to retrieve your purse before he or she proceeds to check you with the hand-held metal detector.

Leaving purses, packages or bags unattended while you're detained and searched by airport security places them at great risk of being stolen. It only takes an instant for a thief to grab your bags and go, especially in a security-check area where there is a lot of rushing and confusion. In fact, security checkpoints in airports are some of the least secure areas for purses and bags.

AT BAGGAGE CLAIM AREAS. At most airports, you're required to present your claim check before you can leave with your luggage. Believe it or not though, some airports do not require you to show a claim check, which means your bags are fair game whenever they come down the chute.

As soon as you get off the plane, proceed directly to the baggage claim area in an effort to be there before your luggage arrives. Even in airports where claim checks are required, in the confusion of the moment when hundreds of people are claiming bags, it's easy for a thief to make off with your bags. So always try to be there waiting when your luggage is ready to be claimed.

WHAT ELSE YOU CAN DO:

- Hold your purse close to your body to make it hard for purse snatchers.

- Try to keep your wallet and airline tickets where a pickpocket can't easily reach them.

- Never carry large amounts of cash if you can avoid it. Carry travelers checks instead.

- Never sleep in a waiting room unless you're traveling with a companion who's awake.

29 SECURE YOUR PURSE BEFORE YOU FALL ASLEEP ON A BUS OR PLANE.

On long trips aboard planes and buses, many people doze and fall asleep. If you're such a person, make sure your purse and bags are secure before you do so. A thief on board could easily help himself to your wallet, remove all the cash, and slip the wallet back into your purse totally undetected. This is especially true on overnight trips where most passengers are sleeping.

There's no easy way to secure your valuables under such conditions. If you put your bags under the seat in front of you (usually as directed by the flight attendant), the person in front of you has as much access to your bags as you do. If you put them in the overhead compartment, everyone coming down the aisle has access to them.

WHAT YOU CAN DO:

- If at all possible, put a lock on all carry-on bags and keep them locked at all times. Use any kind of locking device your purse might have, as well. At the very least, keep your purse zipped tightly shut.

- If you start to doze, try to rest your feet on your bags under the seat in front of you. If someone tries to remove or open your bags, they'll have to move your feet to do it.

- Try to keep your purse in your lap as often as possible. Avoid putting your purse beneath the seat in front of you unless it's absolutely necessary.

- To carry valuables like cash, credit cards, passports and tickets, you can also wear a "neck pouch" (a pouch on a cord that slips around your neck inside your shirt or blouse). Belt pouches also offer a fairly secure place to carry valuables, though not as secure as a neck pouch.
- Don't leave your wallet or tickets in a jacket pocket you store in an overhead compartment.

30. DON'T LEAVE VALUABLES UNATTENDED WHILE YOU PLAY.

It's a common occurrence to see people at the beach run out into the surf, leaving all their valuables by their beach towel. So it's just as common to have a thief come along and help himself to their belongings.

Even if you have your possessions in sight, you might not be able to reach them in time to stop a thief from making off with them. Many thieves are quick and daring. And they don't stop to rummage through bags to see what's inside. They have plenty of time for that after they've made their getaway.

WHAT YOU CAN DO:

- When you go to the beach, take only the things you'll need (food, beverages, sun tan lotion, etc.). Leave jewelry at home or locked in the hotel safe.

- If you take a camera or camcorder, don't leave it unattended while you swim or fish.

- Take as little cash as possible. Carry cash in a waterproof pouch that pins securely to your bathing suit or in a cannister worn around your neck.

- Take everything out of your wallet except for your driver's license. If you need a credit card, take only the one you plan to use. Lock your wallet in the trunk of your car, as concealed as possible.

- Lock all other valuables in the trunk of your car, and carry your key in a waterproof pouch, bathing suit pocket or in a cannister around your neck. Never leave your keys with unattended possessions on the beach. You might lose your car along with everything else.

- Try to park where your car is in plain sight. Keep it locked. And don't leave anything valuable on the seats or dashboard. Lock them in the trunk where they can't be seen.

- If at all possible, have companions with you so that someone will always be with your possessions.

- Never leave purses or packages unattended in restaurants. One of the most common occurrences is at buffets where you have to go through a serving line. Take your purse with you or have a companion wait at the table until you return.

31 NEVER LEAVE VALUABLES IN YOUR HOTEL ROOM WHEN YOU'RE NOT THERE.

Your possessions are extremely vulnerable in hotel rooms. Cameras and camcorders, jewelry, cash, credit cards—even airline tickets can mysteriously disappear from hotel rooms when you go out. Maids and other hotel workers are in and out of your room each day, and while most of these people have been carefully screened for honesty, it's never a good idea to expose them to temptation. But the hotel staff is really the least of your worries.

Your hotel door is wide open while the maid is cleaning. It's easy for a thief to enter while the maid is, say, cleaning the bathroom. It only takes a few seconds for a thief to walk in and quickly gather up your valuables.

It's also relatively easy for an accomplished hotel thief to get his hands on hotel room keys and simply come in while you're gone and take what he pleases.

WHAT YOU CAN DO:

- Always lock your cash, jewelry, credit cards and airline tickets in the hotel safe—not only when you leave your room, but also each night as well.
- Check with the concierge or front desk to determine if the hotel has a safe place to check cameras, camcorders or laptop computers. If not, you're better off taking them with you each time you leave your room.

32 FOLLOW ALL SECURITY WARNINGS IN HOTELS.

Have you noticed all those locks and elaborate security devices on hotel doors? You can bet there's a need for them or they wouldn't be there.

The same is true of signs advising you of security measures to take. There's a need for them, too, so it's wise to heed the warnings.

WHAT YOU CAN DO:

- Always lock your hotel room from the inside the entire time you're in your room. Use all the locks provided. Remember, they wouldn't be there if they weren't needed.

- If your hotel door has a peephole, use it before you open when someone knocks. If you don't recognize the person, don't open the door. Most hotel personnel wear identification badges. If you have any doubts about the person at your door, call the front desk and have them send someone to check out the situation.

- Be sure to lock all your cash and valuables in the hotel safe.

- Carry a portable smoke and intrusion alarm with you and use it while you're in your hotel room.

- Carry a portable travel lock for additional security on your hotel room door.

33 DON'T CARRY A LOT OF CASH WITH YOU.

There's really no need to carry a lot of cash these days. Travelers checks are readily accepted at most tourist destinations throughout the world. So are credit cards.

WHAT YOU CAN DO:

- When you purchase travelers checks, get them in small denominations so you won't get a lot of cash back when making minor purchases.

- Keep your receipt for travelers checks separate from your checks. If checks are lost or stolen, you'll have your receipt as proof of purchase, which can help speed your refund.

- Also, keep a record of each check number you cash along with the date and place you cash it. This will make it easier for the travelers check company to trace any checks written illegally.

- If you have to carry cash when you travel, always lock it in the hotel safe. Don't carry it around with you unless it's absolutely necessary. You also might consider splitting your cash up and carrying part of it in your wallet and part in your pockets. Remember, never "flash" large amounts of cash.

34 TAKE SPECIAL PRECAUTIONS WITH CREDIT CARDS.

Credit card fraud is running rampant. It's imperative that you take certain precautions to avoid becoming a victim yourself.

WHAT YOU CAN DO:

- If you lose a credit card, report it to the issuing bank immediately.

- Every time you use your credit card, tear up all carbons.

- Make sure the credit slip is completely filled out and totalled before you sign it.

- When you get your card back from a waiter or clerk, check to make sure it hasn't been switched with a phony card or one that has expired.

- Never allow anyone to use your credit card number for identification when cashing a check. You're not required to do so. If someone insists that you do, go somewhere else to make the purchase.

- Avoid giving your credit card number over the phone.

- If you have many different credit cards, carry only one or two with you. If your wallet gets lost or stolen, you'll have fewer worries about fraudulent card charges.

- If you have a Personal Identification Number for cash advances on your card, never write it on the back of your card. In fact, try to commit it to memory so you won't have to write it down at all.

PRECAUTIONS TO TAKE IN THE WORKPLACE

The workplace is often referred to as a "home away from home". Today, many husbands and wives both work. In fact, more women are working today than at any other time in our history. The fact that we spend so much time at the workplace may account in large part for the dramatic rise in residential burglaries. And while one group of criminals is busy burglarizing our homes, another group is making its presence felt in and around the workplace. There seems to be no respite from crime regardless of where we are. All we can do is constantly be alert to the possibilities of crime and be prepared to take preventive actions. The following suggestions can help give you a measure of protection against crime during the course of the workday. However, like all the suggestions we have presented, none are foolproof. A desperate or determined criminal can penetrate even the strongest defense.

35 USE CAR POOLS AND VAN POOLS WHENEVER POSSIBLE.

In addition to helping reduce air pollution and lowering the cost of getting to work, car and van pools can give you an extra margin of safety every work day. When it comes to crime prevention, there is indeed safety in numbers.

If you have car trouble on the way to or from work, you won't be stranded on the road alone when you're car pooling. Also, on the days you don't drive, you'll have somebody to drop you off and pick you up in front of your building, so you won't have the worry of parking (possibly in a dark garage) and walking alone to your place of work.

WHAT YOU CAN DO:

- If you work for a large corporation, inquire about van pools. Many large companies have them. They will usually help match you up with other riders who live near you.

- If your company doesn't offer van pools, make some inquiries within the company regarding car pooling.

- Call your local transit authority. In some cities, the transit authority has a program to help match up car poolers.

- Make some inquiries around your neighborhood to try to find someone you trust for car pooling.

- If you don't know the person you'll be sharing a ride

with, and he doesn't work where you do, ask where he works, then call the company to verify his employment. This will at least let you know whether the person has honest employment.

- Be careful about placing ads in newspapers or putting notes on public bulletin boards to locate a car pooler. A rapist or robber could just as easily respond to your ad.

36 EXERCISE GREAT CARE ON PUBLIC TRANSPORTATION SYSTEMS.

Public transportation systems throughout the nation have a good record of protecting riders from crime. Many systems use both uniformed and non-uniformed guards to protect their riders. Also, there are usually other people on board which, to some degree, act as a deterrent.

Your greatest worry isn't so much while you're on the bus or train. Rather, it's the walk to and from your stop and the wait at the stop that exposes you to the greatest danger.

WHAT YOU CAN DO:

- When walking to and from transit stops, try to walk with other people if at all possible.

- Use well-lighted, frequently used stops.

- When exiting the bus or train, be alert to others getting off at your stop. If you feel uncomfortable, quickly walk to where there are other people. If you have to, get back on the bus or train and go to another stop where you feel safer about exiting.

- On a bus, try to sit as near the driver as you can.

- On a train, try to avoid sitting near anyone who looks suspicious. If a transit policeman is on board, sit as near him as possible.

- Hold your purse in your lap with both hands wrapped around it. Don't carry your purse at all if you don't have to have it with you.

- Hold packages in your lap, with your purse sandwiched between your packages and your body.

- When walking to and from transit stops, walk confidently and directly. Stay alert to everything around you. Don't daydream. And never stop to talk to strangers.

- Plan the safest route to and from your transit stop, and always use it.

- Always walk facing traffic, and keep a safe distance from vehicles parked on your side of the street.

- At night, stay away from shrubs, isolated areas, vacant lots and alleys. Stay in lighted areas as much as possible.

- If you are followed on foot, go to a safe place if possible. If you feel threatened, go to a house or business along your route and have someone call the police.

- If you are followed by a car, turn and walk in the opposite direction, and go to a safe place as quickly as possible.

37 BE EXTRA CAREFUL IN PARKING GARAGES, STAIRWELLS AND ELEVATORS.

Just because you reach your place of work with your body and possessions intact doesn't mean you can lower your guard. There could still be danger at almost any turn.

WHAT YOU CAN DO IN PARKING GARAGES:

- Be cognizant of the fact that enclosed parking garages offer plenty of good places for criminals to hide. They can lurk behind concrete pillars and other cars until a victim comes along. Don't let yourself become that victim. Stay alert.

- Always try to park in a well-lighted space.

- Stay alert to suspicious activity as you drive up to your parking space. If you feel uncomfortable about the situation, don't stop. Return to the entrance and report it to the attendant.

- Check out the scene before you get out of your car. If something seems suspicious, stay in your locked car. Return to the entrance and report it to the attendant. If your car is blocked and you can't get out of your parking space, lean on the horn and flash your lights to attract all the attention you can.

- Keep your car keys in your hand until you're safely out of the parking garage. That way, you'll have your keys ready should you have to retreat to the safety of your car for any reason.

- Never stop to answer questions of a stranger. If someone stops his vehicle to ask for directions or information, maintain a safe distance from the vehicle to protect against being grabbed and forced into the vehicle. If the driver or passenger makes an overt move toward you—or makes any kind of sexual innuendo—quickly walk to the building or return to your car and lock the doors. If the person follows you to your car, honk the horn to get attention.

- Avoid walking up or down parking garage stairwells alone. They are often dimly lit and somewhat isolated. If there's no one else around, you may be safer walking up or down the auto ramp where you at least might see someone approaching from the front or either side, and where you could possibly hear someone approaching from the rear. You also have a better escape route on a ramp than you do in an enclosed stairwell. Furthermore, if you have to scream for help, you're more likely to be heard out in the open than you are in an enclosed stairwell. When walking on the ramp, walk as far from parked cars as you can, even if that means walking down the middle of the ramp. However, be sure to watch carefully for cars coming up or down the ramp.

WHAT YOU CAN DO IN BUILDING STAIRWELLS:

- Unless you work in a very secure building where stairwells are regularly monitored by security guards and/or video cameras, it's a good idea to avoid them if you can. Although some people routinely use stairs to get exercise, most people don't. As a result, stairwells are normally pretty lonely places. Also, while you can usually enter the stairwell from every floor, you can't always re-enter the building on every floor from inside the stairwell. Therefore, if you were to encounter a mugger or rapist in the stairwell, you might have to run up or down several flights of stairs before you could get back into the building for help. Even though taking the stairs is good exercise, stairwells are not so good for your personal safety.

WHAT YOU CAN DO IN ELEVATORS:

- While there are usually people in and around elevators in most office buildings, there are still times when you might find them nearly deserted, like after-hours, on weekends or even in the middle of the day in some buildings. You never know when you might find yourself on an elevator with someone who has criminal intent. So make it a habit to stand as close as you can to the floor-selection buttons. If someone threatens you, push the emergency alarm. Also, push as many floor buttons as you can. That will cause the elevator to stop at more floors, increasing your chances of getting help. Also, try to stand with your back against the side wall so you can see other people on the elevator at all times.

38 KEEP YOUR VALUABLES LOCKED UP AT THE OFFICE.

Generally, there is a steady stream of people in and out of most businesses: sales people, delivery people, staff members, and the occasional repairman. Sometimes it is best to keep an honest person honest by not tempting him with your purse, wallet, cash or jewelry.

WHAT YOU CAN DO:

- Always keep your purse and wallet out of sight, preferrably locked in your desk drawer.

- If you take off your watch, earrings or other jewelry during the course of the day, put them in a drawer or cabinet.

- If you remove your coat and hang it up, never leave your wallet in the pocket. Lock it in your desk drawer or keep it in your pants pocket.

- Try to get in the habit of putting all personal valuables in a desk or cabinet when you first arrive each morning. Lock them up and keep the key in your pocket or in a safe place in your office.

- Never leave valuables out in the open or in unlocked drawers when you go on break or leave for lunch.

- Never leave large amounts of cash in your desk drawer or file cabinets, even if they're locked.

- Never leave notebook computers or other small office machines out in the open when you leave for breaks or lunch.

39. KEEP BUSINESS DOORS LOCKED WHENEVER POSSIBLE.

If your office or business only has a few employees and there is little pedestrian traffic, keep the front doors locked whenever it's feasible to do so. In addition, any door not used by customers should be secured during business hours.

WHAT YOU CAN DO:

- Many small businesses install doorbells and remote devices to unlock the door when a customer or visitor rings the bell. This allows people who work in the office to visually screen people admitted to their offices.

- If you arrive early or work late, it's also best to keep doors locked until normal business hours.

- Try to take the same precautions at the office that you do at home. Don't open the door for someone you don't know. When answering the phone and you don't know the caller, never mention that you are alone in the office.

- Never open the door to a stranger who seeks admission before or after regular business hours.

- If you work in a building with security guards, let them know that you'll be in early or late so they can check your offices more frequently.

40. Try to Avoid Keeping a Lot of Cash on Hand at Your Business.

If you own or manage a business that is mainly cash and carry, or if you deal in large amounts of negotiable instruments, try to make bank deposits several times during the day to minimize the amount of cash in the register or safe. Then, post notices at the front door advertising the fact that you don't keep a lot of cash on the premises.

By maintaining only the amount of cash necessary to conduct business, you are accomplishing two goals: one, if a robbery should occur, you'll limit your losses to some degree; two, if there's not a lot of cash in the register, it may discourage the robber from trying to hit you in the future. If a robber strikes it rich the first time, he may come back again.

WHAT YOU CAN DO:

- If it's not feasible to make frequent bank deposits, a concealed safe or hidden drawer are fair alternatives. The important thing is to keep as little cash in the register as possible.

- Always try to maintain "bait" money in the cash register drawer, and keep a record of the denominations, series and serial numbers of the bills. In the event of a robbery, this information can be used by police to help trace the robber.

- Remember, large sums of money are very tempting targets. When you close out the register or count cash, do it in a private area away from prying eyes.

- Above all, if you're confronted by an armed robber, be careful and cooperate. Try to remain calm and be alert and observant. Don't try to be a hero by taking action that could jeopardize your own or someone else's safety.

41 VARY YOUR ROUTINE WHEN MAKING BANK DEPOSITS.

If part of your responsibilities include making daily bank deposits, it's important to be unpredictable in the route and time these deposits are made.

Most robbers look for patterns—a level of consistency that might make a robbery attempt successful. The smart robber will study you closely to try to find a pattern in your routine. If a pattern exists, he will make his plans accordingly.

WHAT YOU CAN DO:

- Try to make the deposits at different times of the day.

- Whenever possible, use a different vehicle and take a different exit from your place of business.

- Carry the deposit in a different satchel, bag or briefcase, and occasionally, let someone else make the deposit (someone you trust, of course).

- If your bank has multiple branches, make it a point to go to different branches from time to time.

- If at all possible, take someone along with you when you make the deposits. The presence of a second person may be just enough deterrent to ward off a would-be robber.

- Another option is to have an armored service company handle your deposits. If this is practical, it is perhaps the safest way to get cash from your business to the bank.

42. MAKE SURE EVERYBODY KNOWS WHAT TO DO IN CASE OF A ROBBERY.

When an armed robbery occurs, there's a great deal of panic and confusion. The robber holding the weapon is usually a desperate person who is nervous and agitated. At the slightest provocation or with one wrong move, the robber may fire his weapon.

To help protect employees and customers alike, it's important that your company have procedures in place in advance. These security procedures should be in writing, and each employee should know them by heart.

WHAT YOU CAN DO:

- Train employees to telephone the police if they observe suspicious behavior.

- Watch out for persons trying to hide on your premises at closing time. Routinely check restrooms and storerooms at closing time.

- If confronted by an armed robber, be cooperative and follow the robber's directions, but do not volunteer more than he asks for.

- Do not make any overt moves. If you have to put your hands in your pockets for a key to the cash register or do anything the robber might misinterpret, explain such actions to him before doing it.

- If the robber hands you a note, place it out of sight and retain it as evidence if you can do it casually without drawing the robber's attention.

- Be as attentive as you possibly can and make as many mental notes as possible. Anything you can recall may help the police in tracking the robber.

- Try to get a look at any vehicles used in the getaway. If you can do it safely, write down the license number, and note the direction in which the robbers fled.

- Call the police immediately.

- Lock all doors and ask any witnesses to remain until the police arrive.

- Write down descriptions of the robbers and other pertinent information immediately.

- Protect the scene of the crime. Don't allow anything to be touched, especially anything the robber may have left behind.

43 MAKE YOUR BUSINESS AS VISIBLE AS POSSIBLE.

Your place of business, like your home, becomes less inviting to criminals when you make it more visible from the street. Good lighting, inside and out, and clear, unimpeded sight lines into the building are two of the easiest and least expensive crime deterrents for businesses.

WHAT YOU CAN DO:

- Proper lighting negates the cover of darkness that burglars prefer. Inside lights around the safe and cash register are particularly important. Outside lights should cover all points of entry, alleys and passageways, especially those in the back of your building.

- It's a good idea to place your cash register close to the front window and keep it well lit at night. Leave it open to show the burglar there's no money inside.

- Valuable merchandise should be kept well away from windows at night, but it should be well illuminated and visible from the street. Try to arrange your merchandise so that a burglar working in a far corner of the store could be seen by someone walking by outside.

- If there is an alarm system, let burglars know. Put decals on the door or window so they are visible from the street.

- Don't provide cover for burglars—or armed robbers. Advertising posters in the window, stacked boxes, vehicles parked in front of windows all partially obstruct the view from outside, making it easier for criminals to work inside.

PRECAUTIONS TO TAKE WHILE SHOPPING

Criminals count on the fact that people are not going to spend their entire lives inside their homes. In fact, we spend a great deal of time outside the home—working, dining out, enjoying recreational activities, shopping and going to school, just to name a few.

It is during the time we are away from home that we are most vulnerable to crime. Therefore, this is the time for greatly increased vigilance and caution. Simply being alert to the possibility of a crime is one of the best defenses we can build around ourselves.

Common sense will tell you that when you're shopping, you become a very attractive target for criminals. You're usually carrying money, credit cards, checks or valuable merchandise. And you usually have to traverse wide open parking areas to get from your car to the store and back again.

Now that you know you're a potential victim, proceed with caution. And concentrate on the situation around you. It'll give you an extra measure of protection every time you're out shopping.

44 LOOK BEFORE YOU PARK YOUR CAR.

Whether it's day or night, familiar or unfamiliar, rain or shine, when you arrive at the shopping center or mall, be on the lookout for anything suspicious before you park your car. It's much safer to take a few extra minutes to survey the parking lot than to simply take the first available space you find.

Many victims are mugged or assaulted in parking areas simply because these areas are generally more isolated. There are fewer people in the parking lot than there are in the mall, so there's less likelihood the assailant will be seen.

Also, there are more avenues of escape for the assailant. A typical mall parking lot has numerous entrances and exits for the criminal to make his escape after attacking a victim.

In addition, the parking lot offers a number of hiding places where the criminal can wait for and surprise his victim. After his attack, he has plenty of places to hide if he can't immediately make his escape.

WHAT YOU CAN DO:

- Never park in a dimly lit section of the parking lot. Most malls and shopping centers are well lighted. Occasionally though, a light is broken or burned out leaving part of the lot in the dark. Don't take a chance and park in a darkened area.

- If you see something suspicious, leave. If you can find

a safe parking space, immediately go inside the store and report the suspicious activity you saw. If you can't park safely, leave. Return home and call the store to report what you saw. It's better to come back another day or shop somewhere else than to take a chance.

- Never park next to a van with double doors on the side. This is the latest thing in traps set by urban gangs. When you step out of your car, gang members hiding inside the van could jump out the side doors and rob, assault or kidnap you with very little risk of being seen. Similarly, if you return from the store to find a double-side-door van parked next to your car, go back in the store and have a security guard accompany you to your car.

- Always make a mental note of where you park! If signs identify the section, write them down if you have to. You don't want to have to wander around a parking lot looking for your car.

45. DON'T SHOP TILL YOU DROP YOUR GUARD.

For some people, shopping is one of life's great pleasures. They'll spend hours in the mall, going from store to store, trying to find that special bargain. Sometimes they get a lot more than they ever bargained for.

As we've said numerous times before, thieves go where there's money—and easy prey. To a mall-weary shopper loaded with packages, fumbling for her keys as she tries to remember where she parked, the thought of being robbed or assaulted is the farthest thing from her mind. But it's foremost in a criminal's mind.

WHAT YOU CAN DO:

- Leave the mall well before closing time. Remember, there's greater safety in numbers. If you wait till closing time when the stores are almost empty, the crowds have thinned out considerably, and you've reduced the number of people who could come to your aid.

- Avoid shopping till you're fatigued. When you're tired you're not as alert. If you're not alert, you could easily become the victim.

- Know exactly where your car is parked. When you park at the mall, take note of the signs that mark the section you're in. Most large shopping centers and malls have signs on light posts designating each area.

- Remember which entrance you used. Malls are large

and sprawling. Sometimes in our confusion, we leave through a different door than we entered. If it happens to be closing time and the door is locked behind you, you might have to walk a long way to get to your car.

- Hold your purse next to your body, with packages covering it. Don't wrap your purse strap around your arm; you could be seriously injured if a robber tries to grab your purse and run.

- If you have children with you, don't let them carry packages. They are defenseless and vulnerable. Hold your child's hand and have him or her walk as close to you as possible.

46 BE ALERT TO ANYONE FOLLOWING YOU OUT OF THE STORE.

Certainly, most people leaving the store when you do will be strangers. And most of them are shoppers just like you. Be alert to them none the less. Watch out for anyone who seems to be paying particular attention to you. This individual could very well be a thief who has marked you as a potential target.

WHAT YOU CAN DO:

- Before you leave the store, look out the door to see if there are people lingering outside. If any of them look suspicious, stay in the store until you can determine what they're doing. They could simply be waiting for a ride; or they could be waiting for the right victim to come along.

- If someone suspicious is about to follow you out the door, stop inside the store and let him go ahead of you. Observe him through the door or window. If he's just another shopper, he'll most likely go to his car and leave. If he's up to no good, he may stop to linger or walk aimlessly in the parking area.

- If you think someone is watching you or following you, don't leave the store. Instead, try to find a security officer and ask him to escort you to your vehicle.

- Never be embarrassed to ask for assistance. Shopping centers and malls provide security not only to protect stores and employees, but also customers. A portion of the price you pay at the store helps pay for this security, much like your taxes pay for police protection. So consider security as something you have bought and paid for. Use it whenever you think you need it!

47. PREPARE TO GET IN YOUR CAR BEFORE YOU LEAVE THE STORE.

The longer it takes you to get from the store to the confines of your car, the greater your exposure to crime. When you're out in the open with nothing between you and a criminal, you have very little protection. You can reduce your vulnerability by following a few simple rules every time you go shopping.

WHAT YOU CAN DO:

- Just before you leave the store, take your keys out of your purse so you'll have them in your hand ready to open the car door.

- If you're right handed, carry your keys in your right hand; if you're left handed, carry them in your left hand. That way, you won't have to shift packages from one hand to the other to unlock the door.

- If you have several packages, put them all into one or two shopping bags while you're still inside the store. That way, you won't have to be fumbling with a lot of packages as you get in your car. (If you know in advance that shopping bags won't be available, take one with you.)

- If you use a shopping cart to carry your purchases to the car, you still should put all items into one or more shopping bags to speed up the process of transferring them to your car.

- Before you leave the store, know exactly where you're

going to put the packages when you reach the car. If you're going to put them in the trunk, do it quickly then get inside your car (after you have looked to make sure no one is hiding inside). If you put packages inside the car, make sure you put them on the floor where they're out of sight.

- Think about where you parked your car. You should know in your mind exactly where it is and how to reach it quickly. If you can't remember where you parked your car, be very careful about wandering around the parking lot looking for it. To be on the safe side, find a security person to help you locate your vehicle. Don't ask a stranger to help you locate it.

48 MAKE YOURSELF A MOVING TARGET.

Like the old saying goes, it's harder to hit a moving target. And when you're out in the open, you should always try to make yourself difficult to be "hit" by a criminal. Given a choice, a thief will almost always take the easiest target.

WHAT YOU CAN DO:

- When you leave the store, walk directly to your vehicle. This is not the time to daydream or wander around the parking lot trying to remember where you parked. When you do, you're giving a criminal an opportunity to zero in on you.

- Walk confidently and at a brisk pace. The amount of time it takes to walk from the store to your car has a direct relationship to the amount of time someone has to approach you.

- As you approach the vehicle, scan the area around and below it. You're looking for anyone lurking behind or beneath your car or a car nearby. If you see anything suspicious looking, do an about face, return to the store and report it to a security guard.

- When you reach your car, quickly look inside. It's possible that someone is hiding on the back seat floorboard waiting for you. Don't unlock the vehicle until you have looked in the front and back.

- If someone approaches you at any time and attempts to

take your belongings, give them to him immediately. Nothing is worth as much as your personal safety. If possible, drop everything on the ground. This will force the criminal to look away from you momentarily, allowing you to back away from the mugger. In most cases, the mugger will quickly retrieve the items and run away. Immediately vacate the area. Either return to the store or leave in your vehicle to file your report with police.

- If your vehicle is unlocked when you return and you're certain you locked it when you left, don't open the door. Return to the store and report it to a security guard.

49 KEEP YOUR PURSE ZIPPED SHUT AND YOUR HAND ON THE ZIPPER.

Leaving a purse open with its contents exposed is like waving a red flag at a bull. Even if you don't happen to be carrying cash or credit cards, you're tempting fate by leaving your purse open. A thief doesn't know what you have in your wallet. He just knows that purses normally contain valuables, so he'll help himself to your wallet and worry about the contents later.

If a thief takes your wallet, he's not only taking your valuables; he's also taking some of your privacy—and possibly some safety away from you and your family. Along with cash and credit cards, your wallet probably has your driver's license with your picture on it, your social security card, pictures of your family, an automatic teller machine card, possibly some blank checks and maybe even a spare key to your home, car, or office. Every one of those items has some value to a thief.

With your driver's license and checkbook, it's possible that he could write a hot check or two on your account. And if he's halfway intelligent, he could probably figure out the Personal Identification Number (PIN) for your ATM banking card. Most PINs are usually the last four digits of either a social security or driver's license number. It wouldn't take some thieves long to figure out how to get money out of your account with both your ATM card and PIN number.

Your driver's license also tells the thief where you

live and what you look like. Family photos might give him clues about your marital status. And if he happens to get lucky and get a key, he'll have everything he needs if he stops by for a visit.

Regardless of whether you carry cash or credit cards in your purse, treat it like the precious possession it is. Keep it zipped shut. And keep your hand on the zipper.

WHAT TO DO IF YOUR PURSE OR WALLET IS LOST OR STOLEN:

- Immediately notify your credit card companies. You should keep a list of all cards and their numbers in a safe place (not your wallet), along with emergency phone numbers to call to report lost or stolen cards.

- If your checkbook gets stolen, immediately go to the bank and close out the account and move the funds into a new account with a different number.

- Immediately report your lost or stolen ATM banking card to the bank.

- Change the Personal Identification Number for your ATM banking card immediately. DON'T USE YOUR BIRTH DATE, ADDRESS, LICENSE NUMBER, TELEPHONE OR SOCIAL SECURITY NUMBER, as these numbers would be readily accessible to anyone who had your wallet. Never write your PIN number on anything you keep in your wallet. Memorize it, and don't tell anyone what it is.

- If your keys are lost with your wallet, change the locks immediately!

- Report your stolen driver's license to the appropriate authority.
- Following the loss or theft of your wallet, be extremely wary of any strangers who come to your home—and watchful of anything suspicious in the immediate vicinity of your home.

50 Beware of a False Sense of Security from Self-Defense Weapons.

In one of the most tragic crimes of 1991 in Houston, an off-duty female sheriff's deputy was abducted from the parking lot of an upscale shopping mall and later murdered. Her abduction occurred at 6:00 in the evening while it was still light. At the time she was abducted, she had a .357 magnum pistol in her purse. Her own gun was used to murder her.

This is not to say the officer was careless or that the gun in her purse gave her a false sense of security. All this says is that any of us could be a victim of crime at any time of the day or night—regardless of how many self-defense courses we have taken or how many defensive weapons we carry with us. The murdered deputy was a well-trained professional who was armed with a high-powered handgun.

We cite her tragedy only to underscore this warning: do not let self-defense weapons diminish your caution or diligence. Do not use them to rationalize what you know to be careless or reckless actions. Otherwise, you could easily be the victim of yet another crime that is just waiting to happen.

We urge you again to think long and hard before deciding to arm yourself. Most law enforcement agencies strongly discourage your carrying a handgun. Not only is it dangerous to you and other people around you, it's against the law in most states. And it could easily be used against you. Unless you know for certain that you could shoot to kill when threatened with bodily harm, you are probably much better off without a gun.

Many citizens have learned Karate and other martial arts to help defend themselves. Still others carry tear gas or electric "stun" guns. If you are going to carry tear gas, make sure it is a good, high-quality product.

Many criminals on our streets today are drug addicts. They have often totally lost touch with reality. This is not the kind of person you want to try to fend off with a new karate move. There is no way to visually determine that a person is in this mental state. Therefore, when it comes to self-defense, there's simply no substitute for concentration, caution and common sense.

Remember!
If you are a victim of a crime, it is NEVER your fault!

Citizens against Crime *"Saving Lives Through Education"*

Defender Plus®
Quality Protection For Your Family's Safety!

A uniquely powerful chemical defense spray that combines CS tear gas, capsicum and ultraviolet dye, all in a solvent base.

Home Model (4 oz.)
with Safety
(Shoots to 12 feet)

Keep in all rooms where you might feel trapped, especially:
- by your bed
- by all doors
- by your shower
- in your car, boat and RV

Personal Model (½ oz.)
with Clip & Key Release
(Shoots to 6 feet)

The clip & key release make it easy to carry:
- in your hand
- attached to your keys
- on your belt
- on your purse strap

Additional Items Available:

Emergency "Call Police" Sign
Light Reflective

For All Cars:
- Gets safe help quickly
- Helps deter criminals
- Keep in your glove compartment

Door & Window Security Stickers
For Homes, Cars, Businesses

For All Doors & Windows:
- Creates illusion of security system
- Helps deter criminals
- Reusable, static cling plastic

What Every Woman Needs To Know... Book

A straightforward, concise book that gives accurate information about sexual assault and practical suggestions for lowering the risk of being the next victim.

Use the order form on the next page to order additional copies of this book and all of the products listed above. **(Note: Prices may vary in your area. Use the toll-free customer service number on the next page for more information.)**

For Fastest Service Call... 1-800-466-1010

NAME _____

ADDRESS _____

CITY _____ STATE _____ ZIP _____

(_____) _____ (_____) _____
DAY PHONE   HOME

	(TAX INCLUDED)	
	QUANTITY	AMOUNT

FAMILY SAFETY PACKAGE .... $135.00 _____ _____
   4 Home Models   (Save $24.95)
   2 Personal Models
   2 Emergency Call Police Signs
   6 Door/Window Security Stickers
   1 *Don't Be The Next Victim* Book

PERSONAL SAFETY PACKAGE ..... $70.00 _____ _____
   2 Home Models   (Save $5.50)
   1 Personal Model
   1 Emergency Call Police Sign
   3 Door/Window Security Stickers

CALL POLICE SIGN PACKAGE ... $25.00 _____ _____
   6 Emergency Call Police Signs   (Save $5.00)

Personal Model w/Key Release .... $20.00 _____ _____

Home Model w/Safety Cap .... $24.00 _____ _____

Door/Window Security Stickers (6) .... $5.00 _____ _____

Emergency Call Police Sign .... $5.00 _____ _____

Personal Model Refill .... $11.00 _____ _____

Don't Be The Next Victim Book .... $6.00 _____ _____
                                                                 (Save $2.95)

What Every Woman Needs To Know Book .... $6.00 _____ _____
                                                                 (Save $1.95)

Shipping & Handling:
- 0 to $10 .... $ 1.35
- $11 up to $35 .... $ 3.50
- $36 up to $81 .... $ 4.00
- $81 up to $134 .... $ 5.00
- $135 & up .... Add 5%

Order Total = _____
UPS Surcharge on purchases
including Home Models only = **$6.00**

➤ Shipping & Handling = _____

TOTAL ENCLOSED = _____

☐ CHECK/MONEY ORDER   ☐ MASTERCARD   ☐ VISA   EXPIRES _____

CARD NUMBER _____ / _____ / _____ /

SIGNATURE _____

Citizens Against Crime
Citizens Against Crime, Inc.
P.O. Box 1241
Allen, TX 75002